TAKING THE PLUNGE

TAKING THE PLUNGE

COMPILED BY
REBECCA CAFIERO

COPYRIGHT © 2024 REBECCA CAFIERO

No part of this publication may be reproduced, stored in a retrieval system, or transmitted in any form or by any means—electronic, photocopying, recording, or otherwise—without prior written permission, except in the case of brief excerpts in critical reviews and articles.

For permission requests, contact the author at rebecca@rebeccacafiero.com

All rights reserved.

Published by Pitch Club Publishing
Cover Design by Jen Rae

ISBN: XXXXXXXXXXX

The author disclaims responsibility for adverse effects or consequences from the misapplication or injudicious use of the information contained in this book. Mention of resources and associations does not imply an endorsement.

This book is dedicated to you, the woman who is READY to take the plunge, to let go and dive into all that is possible!

And especially, this book is dedicated to the brilliant, brave and courageous women of the Pitch Club, who commit daily to the best version of themselves.

CONTENTS

	INTRODUCTION REBECCA CAFIERO	1
ONE	**PLUNGING INTO THE PROCESS** ANGELA TAIT	13
TWO	**PLUNGING INTO THE UNKNOWN** SABRINA STOROZUK	27
THREE	**DON'T GO ALONE** RACHEL WOODWARD	43
FOUR	**MISS-UNDERSTOOD** HARLEY JORDAN	53
FIVE	**THE DIVE INTO DESTINY: NAVIGATING THE WATERS OF CHANGE** PAIGE DUNGAN	65
SIX	**FROM SKYDIVE TO SAFETY NET** MELISSA DEAN	77
SEVEN	**BRIEFCASE TO BABY BOTTLES** BRIGITTE BARTLEY SAWYER	89
EIGHT	**TAKING THE PLUNGE ON ME** AMY BARTKO	99
NINE	**PLUNGING INTO 50** NATALIE BOESE	111
TEN	**PLUNGING INTO THE SACRED** CHRISTINA LUNA	123
ELEVEN	**TAKING THE PLUNGE ON SOBRIETY** MICHELE WATERMAN	141

INTRODUCTION
REBECCA CAFIERO

IN APRIL OF 2022, I was offered an opportunity to co-found a company, in the midst of already owning *two* businesses.

"I've had this idea for years, and I think you're the person to bring it to life," was the invitation made to me by a respected business contact. My curiosity was piqued, and my ego was definitely flattered.

My initial thought was, *'I have no bandwidth to add anything in my life,'* but my curiosity got the best of me. And when I heard the idea, I knew it wasn't one I could pass up. I felt called.

My first question to myself was: is this desire coming from a fear of missing out?

Not making FOMO based decisions was a lesson I had learned well in the form of a miserable year and massive investment lost from a previous startup I'd been involved in.

I was presented the opportunity to invest, and when sharing ideas with the founder, she asked me to join as CEO. My initial intuitive hit was that this particular person wasn't someone I wanted to partner with based on misgivings I had around trust, but I listened to my FOMO of it being a 'billion dollar idea' that'd I'd kick myself for passing up, rather than listening to my own inner alarm.

Starting *any* business is an uphill climb, but starting a business with someone you don't share values with is a sure fire nightmare; hindsight is 20/20. I spent the year feuding with my non-collaborative co-founder while trying to keep our small team motivated and development team on track, long past the writing on the wall screaming at me that this was a lost cause due to the lack of trust, rather than execution. That painful realization resulted in me walking away from both my financial investment and time investment in the company.

The reality is, in a world that often prefers the safety of the familiar and the security of the known, change and taking risks have never been difficult for me. Whether it's attributed to my ADHD or Enneagram 7 personality, or an old pattern from the traumatic forced growth of being financially and logistically on my own my senior year of high school, I'm a firm believer that the only constant in life *is* change.

In fact, a reflection on my last two decades is really a story of the relentless pursuit of change, from moving from rainy Oregon the day after college graduation to the sun soaked streets and opportunities of LA, to the career possibilities of real estate in Vegas, to following a boy and a job in Silicon Valley. Each move wasn't just a change in geography, but a leap into a new chapter of life.

Each transition, each bold decision, was beckoned by the promise of something greater.

INTRODUCTION

"Fear is excitement without the breath," as Fritz Perls said.

Realizing that the same mechanism that creates fear also results in excitement, I've never feared the leap, but breathed in the energy of possible change. My real motivator for change and my real fear has always existed in the reality of stagnation, of not exploring the potential of what could be. Whether it was stepping into the volatile world of entrepreneurship or pivoting from a successful venture into an uncharted domain, my compass has been guided by a singular belief: moving from good to great.

That doesn't mean the leap has always been the "right" choice. That my hope of change leading to a better, happier, fuller, more successful life always results in a positive outcome. Many times, leaping fast has led me deep into some seriously painful lessons, retrospectively ending up in massive growth that I'd prefer not to experience again.

I've realized, it's less about where you're leaping to, than why.

There are now two questions to ask myself before I take any significant leap.

DIVING INTO THE WHY

The first discernment question: Am I running TOWARDS something or AWAY from something?

> "So when you run, make sure you run
> To something and not away from
> 'Cause lies don't need an airplane
> To chase you anywhere"
> **AVETT BROTHERS** - Weight of Lies

I've learned that running away from something only ensures it will catch up to you, no matter where you go. The essence of this lesson? Run towards, not away from. Embrace the pursuit of a calling, not the evasion of discomfort. Make sure it's a plunge, not a bypass.

This discernment is PARAMOUNT.

A fact I know about myself: when I'm in an uncomfortable place where I want to make a change but don't have the courage to face it head on, my tendency is to run. To move, take a new job, leave a relationship. The reality is, we can change our hair, our wardrobe, our home, even our partner, but if we don't change our mindset and behavior, we'll continue to have the same experiences over and over. It's the inward change that is the real change, not the outer.

The wisdom of the plunge is knowing when it is a leap of faith versus a mere escape. It's understanding that not all movements forward are progress if they bypass the essential growth needed to truly evolve.

THE HAPPINESS PARADIGM

The second discernment question: Are you running towards something that is really someone else's, or are you called towards your own evolution?

Chasing someone else's goal of happiness or success will never be the recipe for yours.

I had the painful but valuable gift of learning this at a young age. Even as a "good kid" who had A grades and was the president or captain of most clubs and sports I belonged to, I was also a young changemaker who struggled massively with the iron curtain of my mom and stepdad's parenting style. As a teenager, when I followed my own path to happiness (like choosing cheerleading over a "competitive sport" or self applying to summer leadership camps that meant missing family time), it was often met with criticism and punishment.

During the times of giving in with the goal of making them happy and eliminating conflict, two things happened. I wasn't happy trying to conform to someone else's idea of who I should be, and ultimately, neither were they. It all erupted when doing what I wanted resulted in me coming home from my high school job to garbage bags on the front porch, filled with my clothes.

Navigating the rest of my senior year, college applications, and then working full time while going through college was not easy. It was less of a plunge than a fall, because I didn't have a choice in it, except to give in. Yet I fell forward into a pool of resilience, grit, and resourcefulness that serves me today, 26 years later.

I learned that I'm responsible for my own happiness, no one else's. And I must make decisions from that point.

It's easy to get caught up in the excitement of what someone else is going towards, or to react to someone else's certainty and commitment with an "I should do this too" if you're floundering in your own reality. The distinction between running towards what is truly yours and chasing someone else's dream is subtle yet profound.

I've stumbled down paths illuminated by others' visions, mistaking their enthusiasm for my destiny. But the pursuit of another's definition of success is a voyage with no harbor. When things get hard, if you're running towards a vision that isn't really yours, you won't be able to tap into the courage to move past the fear or challenge. Or, you'll end up at the destination, wondering why it doesn't feel as good as you imagined. It's a lesson in understanding that the authenticity of your journey is what crafts a life of fulfillment.

My husband once said to me, "Do what you can to be happy, because when you're happy, you can do anything."

I realized that's been my mantra of how I've lived life. This philosophy has underpinned every plunge I've taken, teaching me that even in the face of failure, there is an evolution, a metamorphosis that is intrinsically valuable. Pursue happiness with fervor, for it is the foundation upon which all else is built.

When you know that you're being called towards something that is truly yours, you will be faced with the fear of change, of failure. Even if your efforts "fail", it's about the evolution of who you are, of where you're going. It's about plunging in and what you learn from that plunge. When you take the plunge, it's a transition from the known world to the unknown world. All the growth lives there.

Whether you choose to take a leap or you choose to stay where you're at, taking the plunge is not merely about the act itself but about the aftermath, the sitting in the discomfort of new waters, and realizing that this discomfort is a catalyst for growth. It's about understanding that the slow numb of stagnation is far more excruciating than the shock of new beginnings.

LETTING GO TO GROW

Sometimes, the plunge doesn't make sense, but you jump in faith. You can't know all the answers. You have to trust your intuition. It's an invitation to embrace your own transitions, to recognize the power of plunging into the unknown, and to discover the profound growth that lies in the depths of uncertainty.

One of the greatest challenges in life is not the act of plunging into the unknown but the willingness to let go of the old version of ourselves. It's a realization that the birth of our new selves is predicated on our willingness to leave behind the familiar. The plunge, then, is not just a leap into the unknown but an initiation into a new existence.

The plunge is the initiation. The evolution.

THE LITMUS TEST OF DECISIONS

In moments of indecision, when the weight of potential paths bears down with unbearable heaviness, I've found solace in a simple practice: "decide" before you sleep, and let the dawn bring clarity. This ritual, of waking up with a decision as if it were already made, has often been the clearest indicator of what path my heart truly desires. If I feel relief and excitement, the decision was the right one. If I feel regret, it wasn't. With that clarity, I can move forward in aligned action.

Back to the opportunity I'd been presented with….

I asked myself, *Am I running TOWARDS something or AWAY from something?*

I knew I wasn't running away from anything. I had a successful business I loved, where I was living in a centerpoint of what I was great at, what was needed, what I enjoyed, and was being paid well for. Yet under the surface, I'd been struggling with the question of scaling for a while. I knew I was meant to impact in a bigger way, but wasn't ready to give up *really* good for an unknown great.

I had a million reasons not to pivot to something new, in an industry I was unfamiliar with, with a business partner who I'd known briefly. Yet I felt that this was my greater purpose, the evolution of my mission and impact.

The Second Question: ***Are you running towards something that is really someone else's, or are you called towards your own evolution?***

While I didn't gestate the idea, when I added my mission driven wish list to it, The Compassion Collective was born.

A clean beauty + lifestyle product company.

Sustainability focused.

Wth a give back angle.

The problem Compassion Collective solves was one I'd been unconsciously working towards for years, on the sidelines.

Helping families impacted by cancer.

I lost my boyfriend 14 years ago to cancer. I'd been through it again with my husband. Both experiences rocked me and changed who I am. They led me into entrepreneurship, to have more freedom over my schedule when I had to make tough choices between hospital visits and required meetings. They inspired me to create scholarships in my communities, donating, and having fundraisers to non-profits.

Instead of using my main focus of my primary business, coaching female founders, to give me the funds and ability to create impact as a hobby, building Compassion Collective is an opportunity to make a massive impact, while doing immeasurable good through products that are good for people, for community, and for the world. To make my mission my main focus.

I didn't need to hear more. I *leaped*.

AFTER THE LEAP

Despite my whole hearted *yes* to the Compassion Collective, my initial approach was tentative, a mere dipping of the toe rather than the full-bodied plunge. I found myself caught in a familiar trap, convincing myself of a lack of bandwidth when, in truth, it was an invitation to realign my priorities and make the necessary sacrifices to embrace this new chapter.

As the universe would have it, my hesitance was met with a series of unexpected challenges. These were not mere obstacles but tests of my resolve. The Compassion Collective, while it began to flourish with ease, and opportunities seemed to align perfectly, it demanded more than I was ready to give, not in time, but in focus. My commitment to restructure my existing business, to simplify parts of it while I dedicated more of myself to this new endeavor, faltered. I failed to make the hard choices, to truly prioritize this new path over the comfort of the old. And the universe forced me to make them, often painfully.

The result? I stripped away the parts of my life and business that were egoic or not working, rather than led by heart. I released obligations that felt like weight, even though it caused short term pain and discomfort. On the other side of that? Space for my evolved mission.

It was a poignant lesson in commitment and the importance of wholeheartedly embracing the opportunities that align with our deeper purpose. The challenges that arose served as a stark reminder that half measures would not suffice. The universe, in its infinite wisdom, was urging me to take the leap fully, not just for the sake of The Compassion Collective but as a testament to my own evolution.

This experience, though fraught with discomfort, was a catalyst for profound growth. It reinforced the lesson that when we encounter opportunities that resonate with our soul's purpose, we must not only approach them with curiosity and openness but with an unwavering commitment to dive in, fully and fearlessly. It's about making space, not just in our schedules, but in our hearts and our lives, for the transformations that beckon us forward.

Are you ready to let go of the old you, realizing that the new you is only born in the plunge?

TO MY EARLIER SELF: A LETTER ACROSS TIME

Dear Rebecca,

As you stand on the precipice of countless plunges, both seen and unseen, I offer you this counsel: Embrace every leap with an open heart and a fearless spirit. Understand that the true essence of life lies not in the safety of the shore but in the exhilarating depth of the sea. Trust in the journey, for it is in the act of plunging that you will discover your true strength, your true purpose, and, ultimately, your true self.

Remember, it is not the certainty of the outcome that defines the value of the plunge but the lessons learned, the resilience built, and the joy of discovering that, with every leap, you are capable of far more than you ever imagined.

ABOUT
REBECCA CAFIERO

Rebecca Cafiero is a TEDx Speaker, international Forbes contributor, and six-time bestselling author. She is also the host of the top-ranked podcast, Becoming You. Rebecca's expertise has been featured in prominent media outlets including NBC News, ABC News, US News and World Report, Reader's Digest, Women's Health and more. She lives in the Bay Area, California, with her husband, two children and golden retriever.

As a business founder and life strategist, Rebecca specializes in helping female entrepreneurs intentionally grow their businesses without sacrificing their quality of life. As the founder and CEO of The Pitch Club, a seven figure, for women & by women company, she has helped thousands of women across the globe achieve milestones like doubling their income in a year, receiving dozens of media mentions, and taking at least a month of vacation each year.

CHAPTER ONE
PLUNGING INTO THE PROCESS

ANGELA TAIT

AS VINCENT VAN GOGH ONCE SAID, 'Great things are not done by impulse, but by a series of small things brought together.' Reflecting on my journey, I've come to understand the profound truth in these words. My path, initially marked by impulse, gradually evolved into intentional strides that changed my very essence. This shift didn't just alter my trajectory, it realigned my purpose, passion, and power.

In the early stages, my actions were driven by immediate desires and reactions, much like the impulse van Gogh speaks of. Yet, as I ventured further, the realization dawned upon me: true growth and achievement lie not in the grandiose leaps, but in the nuanced, deliberate steps taken day after day. This understanding prompted a deep plunge into the process of personal and professional development, an adventure where each step, no matter how small, was a building block for something greater.

This shift to embrace the process became the crucible in which my purpose was redefined. No longer adrift in the whims of impulse, I began to see a clear vision of what I was meant to achieve. My passion, too, found a deeper, more resonant expression. It was no longer about fleeting enthusiasms but a sustained fire, fueled by the small victories and lessons learned along the way. And from this, my power emerged — not as a force of dominance but as the strength to influence, to create, and to inspire.

Delving deep into the process revealed the intricate beauty of persistence and adaptability. Each challenge faced, each setback overcome, and each milestone reached added layers to my understanding and capabilities. It taught me that the true meaning of achieving greatness lies in the accumulation of experiences, the willingness to learn, and the courage to persist.

I now understand the beauty of persistence and adaptability. The willingness to learn. The courage to continue when you want to walk away. Each challenge faced, each setback overcome, and each milestone reached. These experiences are what it means to achieve greatness. Purpose is discovered in pursuit, passion is ignited in action, and power is built in perseverance. Through this lens, every aspect of the process becomes a step toward actualizing the greatness that van Gogh envisioned; a greatness crafted not by the allure of immediate results but by the profound impact of small, purposeful actions woven together over time.

As we delve into the nuances of my journey, remember that it is this experience of the process, this deep plunge into day-to-day dedication, that has sculpted the person I am today. It is here, in the meticulous commitment to growth, that my purpose was clarified, my passion intensified, and my power truly realized.

THE TURNING POINT

It was a sunny day in Southern California and I was next to a window sitting at my desk. I was browsing through different master degree programs when I discovered the Master of Science in Organization Development (MSOD) at the business school of Pepperdine University.

As I went page to page to learn more about the program, I got goosebumps as I scrolled through the website on my computer; everything I was reading about the two-year program was exactly what I needed and wanted in a grad school program. The program promised not just education, but transformation through international collaboration and quarterly intensives worldwide, like China, Costa Rica, France and throughout the US. It was a virtual grad school with a cohort from all over the world. I would be able to continue working to support myself because of the flexible schedule, while learning at my own pace. They had assigned reading, virtual lectures, team calls, and more, allowing for both independent and group work. Only thirty people were accepted into the program every year.

The deadline to apply for Fall 2013 was coming to a close in a matter of weeks from when I came across the program. I did everything I could to get my application in on time. I was in action mode and was looking for the fast track to get in right away. As the weeks and months passed, I anticipated finding out more about my submission. I would check the mailbox, my email, and reach out to my contact at the school to see if there were any updates. It was crickets, my anxiety heightened, and I was getting worried in anticipation.

FAILING FORWARD

It turns out the worry was warranted. My application to my dream program was rejected. There I was, standing at the edge of what felt like the biggest failure of my life. My impulsive strategies had led me to a dead end. Little did I know, this moment of defeat was about to teach me the most valuable lesson of my life: the transformative power of leaning into the process.

I immediately put my problem-solving skills into place to figure out next steps to explore how to get into the program with the next application cycle. I ended up meeting with the Dean of the MSOD program at a coffee shop in San Clemente, California to learn more about what I could do to get into the MSOD program. I emphasized to the Dean my desire and hopes to be part of something that felt so magical and promising for my personal and professional growth. She mentioned resources, informational calls, classes, certifications, and other options to consider getting more experience in the field since I was coming from a sales background and had very little experience in organization development. As soon as our meeting ended, I went to work and started setting up one-on-one calls with alumni, enrolling in classes, becoming part of networking groups, and more. As I dove deeper into the process, it solidified my desire for the program and my alignment of what it offered. The alumni calls were informative in preparing me for my journey ahead, offering recommendations for who else to connect with from the school, what other networks and classes to look into. These initial meetings were little bread crumbs leading me closer to the house from the forest. Now, I had a clear direction of my path forward to get into my dream program and school. As I continued learning and growing, I followed up with the Dean and others to educate them on everything I had been doing over the last year to better prepare and equip myself for the challenges ahead.

THE FULL CIRCLE MOMENT

Months passed. I was living in San Diego. Things had changed in my personal life, but this goal remained steady. I was driving on The 5 in San Diego and I received a phone call from an unknown number. It was to tell me that I was accepted into the MSOD program for the Rho Prime class.

As I hung up the call, I was speechless that all my hard work, dedication, calls, meetings, classes, and even the first rejection, had truly and epically paid off. It was a moment so indescribable: tears of joy, love, and excitement streamed down my face. Growing up I was bullied for not being 'smart' and this moment not only proved to myself, but I thought it would prove to others that I didn't have to continue fighting to show my worth.

I pushed beyond what I thought was possible, I took a chance on myself knowing that I deserved more, I could do better and I was capable. I was amazed and proud of myself for committing to the process to continue growing. I had validated my passion for the program, the curriculum, and the school. I did not let the initial rejection hold me back in the long run.

The program was everything I thought and more. It had students from Australia, Dubai, Europe, and the US. We traveled, partnered with companies around the world, solved real life issues taking place in real organizations, and one of my teams even got a chance to talk with the government in France on sustainability efforts in the US. After graduating from the program in 2016, I was still passionate about the program and became a brand ambassador. I did a photoshoot for the Pepperdine Business School website to attract future applicants to the MSOD program. At one point I had my picture in various spots throughout the business school website. Another year went by, and the business school reached out to do another photoshoot, this time my picture was on billboards across Los Angeles marketing the business school.

I thought back to the anguish I felt after being denied during that first application cycle in 2012. Seeing my face on billboards in 2018 advertising Pepperdine was a full circle moment; 2012 me never would have imagined what was in store and that I would get accepted into such a prestigious school, let alone be the cover girl for its prestige and brilliance.

Every time I saw one of those billboards or my picture on the website, it reminded me of the incredible experiences I had in the program and gave me a sense of gratification for the thousand steps that I took to get accepted. It was also a reminder that sometimes you need to trust the process, take the plunge on the road less traveled, and go for what you want in life.

FROM SALES TO HR: A NEW BEGINNING

In a flash, I graduated from my dream program with a great education and made the transition from a decade in sales to a career in Human Resources. When I began my career in sales, I never would have anticipated how difficult it would be to pivot into HR. Stepping into recruiting and HR helped me to fully dive into helping leaders build efficient and effective teams where culture matters, and their employees feel a sense of purpose and value.

When I look back, though, I realize that sales was a bridge and a stepping stone that I never anticipated. I graduated with my undergrad in media management, thinking I was going into casting, production or directing. After living in Los Angeles and interning at different networks, I realized that was not the career for me. My shift into sales was not unfounded. In the end, everything is sales; it's just a question of what you're selling.

I didn't realize at the time that the same lessons that I learned in my job in sales, and that I put into practice in order to get accepted into graduate school, still needed a lot of practice and fine tuning.

There is a term used in Hollywood that every actor wants to avoid: typecasting. An actor who is typecast is one who scored their first big role, but one that highlighted a unique quality or quirk that had the side effect of creating a perception that they weren't a good fit for other types of roles. The personality or skills become pigeonholed into one type of role.

Even with a master's degree in organizational development, employers looked at my experience in the workforce and immediately saw me as a candidate for sales positions, which was not what I was looking for. I had been professionally typecasted. Fortunately, I had been through rejection before, and I had learned that the answer wasn't giving up or chasing after some new, shiny opportunity.

Despite doubts from potential employers about my experience, I remained persistent. I started with jobs that most of my graduate program peers were landing and often required an advanced degree like mine. But I didn't have real world experience in the field, so I was underqualified. I applied for entry level positions, but my degree meant I was overqualified. I felt like I was in a pickle. Through the process of many interviews, followed by many rejection letters or emails, I hung on. This resilience was now in my blood after what I experienced when Pepperdine turned me down. It was that process, and the lessons I learned from it, that, more than my degree, actually would lay the foundation for my success.

Have you ever found yourself, like me, at a crossroads where you've hit some obstacle and start to really see the grass on the other side of the fence looking suddenly much more green? What if I told you that the key to unlocking your greatest achievements lies not in the grand leaps, but in the small, deliberate steps you're hesitant to take?

It took around three years of interviews and change to finally land an internal job as a Recruiter. Getting to this step was a process in itself. Previously interviewing for HR and organization development roles, multiple hiring managers did not think I had enough experience. They told me it would take more work to train me rather than hiring someone that came from a typical HR background. When I finally received an offer for a full time recruiter, I was also taking a pay cut on my base salary; the role was mostly commission based. I worked hard to build up my clientele and learn my role inside and out to make a positive impact.

My big break came when a prospective client mentioned to me that they needed someone in HR and were interested in what

I was able to provide. I leaned into the opportunity and I helped grow their company of 10 employees to over 100 in less than two years. I handled every aspect of HR and eventually was able to grow a team under me to support the growth.

After working at the company for a few years, it was time to open a new chapter of being my own boss. I had learned so much, and I was ready to spread my wings. I decided it was the right time to start my own HR Consulting and Recruiting business called Tait Consulting, LLC.

The organization supports other candidates that might experience what I went through, as well as empowers leaders and small business owners to sustainably scale to the next level by hiring top talent, training employees, and providing business coaching. Becoming a successful small business owner was not straightforward. It involved setbacks, learning curves, and ultimately, the realization that every experience, every rejection, was a step towards my goals.

I've always had resilience, however my persistence to move my career into HR put my track record of resilience into practice. My determination and grit to not give up on a career I knew I wanted eventually led to a business that I'm motivated to work on every single day.

LET'S GET TO THE GOOD STUFF

We live in a world obsessed with instant results, where the process is often seen as a mere obstacle to our goals. Yet, I've discovered that the process itself is not just a pathway to success; it's the very foundation of it. Often, we want to skip to the good part, go all the way from step one to steps eight, nine, or even ten.

In our quest for achievement, we often glorify the grand leap. The singular, momentous decision that propels us from where we stand to where we dream to be. This leap is seen as a pivotal point of transformation, an instant when everything changes. Yet, beneath the surface of these leaps lies a deeper, more powerful force at play: the relentless, meticulous plunge into the process.

It is this immersive dive into the everyday, the routine, and the minutiae that truly crafts the foundation for extraordinary results. Imagine, for a moment, an artist standing before a blank canvas. The masterpiece does not emerge from a single stroke of brilliance but from thousands of deliberate, thoughtful applications of paint. Each brushstroke represents a decision, a moment of reflection, a choice to adjust, refine, or boldly reimagine. Similarly, in the fabric of our own ambitions, it is not the sweeping gestures but the intricate stitching of daily efforts, learning, and perseverance that shape our greatest achievements.

Consider the process as a river carving its way through a landscape. At first glance, its power might seem subdued, its progress slow and meandering. Yet, over time, this persistent flow sculpts canyons, nurtures ecosystems, and reshapes entire terrains. It is the consistent, sometimes imperceptible pressure, the water's unyielding contact with rock and earth, that leads to monumental change. Our own journeys are much the same. It is through the steady accumulation of experiences, the continuous application of effort to obstacles, and the relentless pursuit of improvement that we achieve our most notable results.

PLUNGING INTO THE PROCESS

This deep plunge into the process requires courage. It demands that we shift our focus from the distant horizon to the ground beneath our feet, from the outcome to the action. It asks us to find value in the trials and to embrace the incremental advancements with as much enthusiasm as the leaps. It's in this immersive engagement with our goals that we discover not just the path to success but the resilience, adaptability, and insight that are the true rewards of our endeavors.

In essence, while the grand leaps may define our direction, it is the deep, dedicated plunge into the process that propels us forward, ensuring that when we do arrive at our destination, we are not just triumphant but transformed. It's here, in the granularity of our efforts, that the potential for greatness truly lies, waiting to be unlocked by those willing to dive deep and embrace the journey in all its complexity.

When we have a big goal in mind, it can be hard to understand the full vision clearly since we are so focused on the specific outcome. As we get closer to the finish line, however, more begins to unfold in a miraculous way. We start to see how each chapter along the way was so monumental to the final version that comes to fruition, even if the small steps feel mundane or useless in the moment.

Sometimes we need to go slow to move fast. By allowing space and freedom, more options can come into our life that take us to a place we never thought possible, which is truly a remarkable experience to endure. So, listen to your heart, embrace the road less traveled, and remember that even though you may feel like it is taking a long time to reach the top of the mountain, you could be a couple steps away from your next big achievement.

EMBRACING THE JOURNEY: FROM CURIOSITY TO CREATION

My odyssey from the initial leap into the MSOD program to establishing Tait Consulting encapsulates a pivotal transformation. It wasn't merely about achieving milestones but discovering resilience, learning, and evolving every step of the way by leaning into the process. This expedition has been less about the destinations reached and more about valuing resilience in setbacks, the insights from each doubt, and the unforeseen paths that led to new horizons.

Victory, I've learned, is sculpted not only through the achievements but through the rich tapestry of experiences that shape our character, broaden our skills, and refine our goals. It's in the climbs, filled with challenges and serendipity, where true transformation unfolds — shifting my perception of success from a series of outcomes to a journey enriched by every step, decision, and pivot.

As I reflect, I invite those at a crossroads, teetering between decision and change, to embrace the journey with an open heart. It's in this dance of intention and adaptability where we find our authentic selves, not merely by aiming for the landing but by cherishing the flight of discovery and growth. Each plunge into the process can lead to moments of gratitude and success that create a life beyond what seems possible.

In the spirit of moving forward with intention and reflection, I challenge you to take a moment to journal about your journey. Write down the milestones you've achieved, the obstacles you've navigated, and the lessons you've learned. Reflect on where you currently stand in your adventure and identify your next step. Let this exercise not only serve as a testament to your progress but also as a roadmap for the journey ahead. Remember, the power of change lies in each deliberate action, no matter how small. So, take this challenge to heart, set your intentions, and boldly step forward, knowing each foot placed in front of the other moves you closer to your aspirations. Let's not just dream of impact—let's plan for it, one thoughtful step at a time.

ABOUT
ANGELA TAIT

Angela is an internationally recognized HR and Talent Development Leader with over 10+ years of experience facilitating strategic growth for small, mid, and large corporate teams. Though her experience has spanned a diverse array of industries, some of her most notable work includes training and growing staff by 1000% within 2-years, as well as increasing employee 90-day retention by 80%.

Beyond her field experience, she is a board member on AZ Organization Development Network (ODN), holds a Society of Human Resource-Certified Professional (SHRM-CP) Certification, and has a Masters Degree in Organization Development from Pepperdine University. Today, she is the CEO and Founder of Tait Consulting, a HR Consulting and Recruiting firm, which supports growth-minded leaders to lower turn over, increase revenue and sustainably scale to the next level by hiring top performers, coaching executives, and building employee development systems.

CHAPTER TWO
PLUNGING INTO THE UNKNOWN

SABRINA STOROZUK

NAVIGATING THE TECH INDUSTRY AS A WOMAN is not for the faint-hearted, yet I'm consistently drawn to the challenge. In a field predominantly occupied by men, we're often left to fend for ourselves — learning to not just survive but to flourish amidst frequent interruptions, belittlement, and underestimation in an arena where debates on our intelligence, character, and worth are a public spectacle. Even the simplest act of belonging is contested, with skeptical glances that question our presence, especially if we defy the expected image.

Every day, as women, we have to transcend these barriers: maintaining composure, exhibiting charm, wit, and intelligence, all to carve a place at the table among the 'big boys.' It's at this table where I set my sights.

Determined to stand my ground in this ruthless landscape, I founded an IT solutions and services company. For a decade, I spearheaded complex, transformative projects globally, ranging from fledgling startups to Fortune 500 corporations. Concurrently, I plunged into various ventures, channeling my passion for resolving intricate problems — a fascination that became my signature trait.

I earned recognition as a thought-leader, sharing my insights on tech startups and entrepreneurship at eminent universities, and contributing to expert panels at major industry conventions. My tenacity and dedication to my craft defined my career path. But what was the cost of this relentless drive?

My path through life's trials has been paved with resilience, a quality that has allowed me to endure hardships with grace. This resilience was my shield against the twists and turns of fate. Until one day, it wasn't enough.

My ceaseless drive towards my goals demanded a pace that was nothing short of relentless, one that I upheld for far too long. This all-consuming chase after achievement ultimately led to multiple severe burnout incidents, which I light-heartedly dubbed "spa days," though they were anything but relaxing. These moments were desperate warning signs from my body, signaling that anxiety and exhaustion was inching me perilously close to the edge of my very existence.

Concealed behind a masquerade, my true self had become obscured, eluding grasp. I faced the daunting task of reclaiming my identity, a task requiring deep introspection and a steadfast dismantling of self-imposed boundaries. The key to rediscovering my former essence had slipped from my hands. Without the necessary instruments, ensnared by constant distractions or overcome by exhaustion, the process of stripping away pretenses to uncover the genuine 'me' appeared unattainable.

Yet, this narrative, my narrative, reaches beyond a single individual. It heralds a broader saga of grit and metamorphosis among women in the tech industry and women pursuing the life they were destined to have. Our collective story is elevated by the powerful testament of our perseverance through adversity and our extraordinary ability to forge our paths, even under the weight of seemingly impossible barriers.

THE COCOON SEASON

Enter my "cocoon season," the season I endured the most professionally grueling years of my life; years I think of as lost. It all began with a venture that consumed every ounce of my passion, time, and finances for three years, only to crumble before my eyes in a mere three months when COVID-19 emerged. This project wasn't just a business; it was the dream everyone clamored to join, pour money into, and touted as the next big unicorn — an initiative worth billions, or so we all believed.

I had envisioned this venture as my rocket ship to the summit of the tech industry, positioning me shoulder to shoulder with the giants. But when it imploded, the weight of that failure crashed down on me with a brutal force that was more than humbling, it was crippling. The price of my ambition was steep; in its pursuit, I sidelined the first precious year of my son's life. While I was physically there, my mind was absent, invested in work: work I believed was all for the right reasons.

The financial loss, paradoxically, was the easier pill to swallow; money could be re-earned, but time was irrevocable. What sliced through me was the epiphany that my relentless drive had inadvertently cost me moments with my child. That realization delivered a deep, searing pain. I had been toppled over by circumstance, and for the first time, I found myself unwilling to stand back up. I faced an identity crisis of seismic proportions; the future I had so meticulously planned for had evaporated, and with it, my will to rebuild.

Utterly spent and seeking refuge from the relentless entrepreneurial grind, I yearned for evenness, for time unburdened by ambition with my family, for unadulterated simplicity. I longed to live free from the relentless weight of expectation and pressure. All I desired was to simply *be*. Quietly present, available, and immersed in the very existence I had nearly sacrificed on the altar of success.

METAMORPHOSING INTO A STRANGER

In need of respite from the start-up whirlwind, I plunged into the corporate sphere, seeking solace and recuperation. This corporate detour, paradoxically, represented my notion of 'slowing down.' Inside corporate's methodical cadence, I aimed to reclaim my vitality, mental capacity, and essence while picking up new skills along the way.

A chance encounter at a dinner led to an unexpected job offer. It came with a hefty salary and tempting benefits, complete with a title that satiated my desire for recognition but, crucially, not one that heaped on me a cumbersome load of administrative tasks, office politicking, or overbearing leadership responsibilities. My mantra was simplification: concentrate on one role, one area of expertise. This was liberating, at least for the first half of the year, dovetailing with our earnest plans to grow our family.

However, after the six-month honeymoon phase, feelings of stagnation and discontent began to surface. Each day felt like an infinite loop; Groundhog Day on repeat. With the added sting of being expected to toil beyond my mandated hours without any share in equity. The confines of the corporate world, a predictable 9 to 5 existence, started to chafe against my nature. My drive for innovation, change, and true problem solving. Despite feeling increasingly out of sync, I held on, believing in seeing through this chapter beyond a mere year, even as I likened my efforts to a Sisyphean ordeal.

I could sense my identity fading; apathy settled in, along with a sense of mediocrity that I abhorred. In search of greener pastures, I switched jobs repeatedly, only to discover a bleaker landscape at each turn. The final stint felt akin to an inhospitable desert where growth and prosperity were impossible — a marked contrast to my teenage job at a psychiatric hospital's kitchen, which by comparison seemed blissful.

I ventured into myself, only to emerge as someone still far removed from who I aspired to be. I was in the wrong place for all the seemingly right reasons.

Amid a career continually marred by poor leadership, toxic environments, and corporate machinations, my spirit grew heavy, leading to a pervasive, yet functional, depression. Meanwhile, my personal life was upended by a harrowing sequence of familial health crises and losses — from the passing of my grandfather, to my beloved great aunt Lena, and then my cousin's husband, Tom.

Among these tragedies, the most soul-shattering was my grandmother's; my "Nanny" or "Nan," diagnosed with lung cancer. Since childhood, I've recognized the rarity of a soul like hers — a once-in-a-lifetime alignment of stars. She was the centerpiece of my emotional support system, my guiding star. The fear of her absence, a foreboding shadow since my youth, became a grave reality. I worried that without her, my very foundation would shatter, unraveled by the loss of control over my emotions, the facade of strength and resilience I presented, and my skill in compartmentalization. I had braced myself for this heartache, knowing its impact would be profound, and when it arrived, it broke me in ways I had long apprehended.

MY SECOND LIFE CYCLE

On March 8th, 2023, a profound loss tore through my world. My beloved Nan, Rita Amero, passed away. This was not just a day of mourning, it was the day I commenced my metamorphosis again, transitioning from a protective cocoon into the freedom of butterfly wings. Beneath the weight of this ruthless grief, I found the impetus to start anew. The intensity of the loss was overwhelming, exposing depths of emotion and vulnerability that I had never encountered, and in doing so, it reset my entire worldview.

With every heartbeat, I yearned to embody the essence of my Nan. She was a beacon of inner beauty and grace. A light that shone brilliantly, touching everyone with her generosity, wit, and unquenchable zest for life. To those in need, she offered everything: her time, her wisdom, the comfort of her presence, often sacrificing her own needs without a second thought or the expectation of anything in return. She navigated life on her terms, seizing each moment with joy and wholehearted appreciation, making every individual feel cherished and personally significant.

Her calendar brimmed not with her own affairs but with the milestones of others — a reminder to celebrate alongside them, to share in their joy tangibly, whether through a thoughtful note, a loving call, or a heartfelt gift. This kind of selflessness made everyone feel like she was "their person." My newfound aspiration to mirror such profound humanity felt like a calling that resonated with my soul.

Through this came a moment of clarity I experienced which was transformative, acting as a catalyst for profound self-discovery and release. It marked the beginning of shedding the person I thought I was supposed to be, embracing instead the profound insights my grandmother had shared with me throughout my life. This realization led to immediate and significant changes in my behavior, which may have seemed unexpected to those around me, but were deeply aligned with my core instincts. As I stood metaphorically at the brink once more, ready to take the plunge into the unknown, I found myself hesitating — not out of fear, but from a desire for deeper understanding.

This time, my approach was different. I wasn't looking for quick solutions. Instead, I sought to uncover the root causes of my challenges, to ensure that my future choices would be informed by genuine insight rather than fleeting desires. I turned my natural inclination for unraveling complex issues towards introspection, delving into my motivations with the aim of comprehensively understanding myself.

Through meticulous reflection and analysis of my experiences, I identified key insights that illuminated my path forward, guiding my decisions with newfound clarity and purpose. This plunge into uncharted waters wasn't just about making changes; it was about understanding why those changes were necessary, anchoring my actions in the wisdom that had been passed down to me and the deep self-awareness I had cultivated.

Following this revelation, I took decisive action. I left behind outdated ways of thinking, opting for intuition over strict logic breathing new life into the term reprogramming. I embraced complex challenges beyond the realm of technology. This wasn't just about personal growth; it extended to how I interacted with the world, shifting from chasing individual success to contributing to our collective well-being. I started to go with the flow more, easing up on my need to control everything and making space for downtime, which brought a healthier balance to my life. Little did I know, this plunge into the unknown, this dedication to finding myself and reframing my perspective on work, were the foundational stepping stones I needed to be able to flourish in my next chapter.

This shift led me to start a new project, focused on empowering women. It's more than a business; it's a mission to offer support, liberation, and hope for a better future. This venture stands as a testament to my transformation, marrying my skills and passions to uplift others. It's about creating opportunities for women and fostering a community where we all move forward together. This step not only changed my direction but also aimed to light the way for others, emphasizing collaboration, empowerment, and shared achievements.

Every change, every new decision seemed to orchestrate itself flawlessly, as if destiny had laid out a path for me to follow. This shift in perspective marked a stark contrast to my past self — one driven by logic and efficiency rather than heart and intuition. The Sunday scaries vanished, replaced by autonomy and a powerful network of inspiring entrepreneurs. Now, moving at a gentler pace, I could savor the journey, nurturing both my personal well-being and professional connections.

LEARNING TO FLY: THE BUTTERFLY SEASON

This season marks a pivotal point in my path: I'm shifting from merely talking about change to actually making it happen. I'm putting into practice the changes I've aimed for, living by my principles, and actively pursuing my ambitions. A critical realization that struck me, and is often highlighted by my partner, is the importance of teamwork in any endeavor. Despite once taking pride in going alone, believing collaboration might slow me down, I've started to see things differently. I wondered, what if I had embraced teamwork earlier? Could combining forces have propelled my projects further, faster? Would having a supportive circle have eased the burdens I carried alone, making even the challenging times more manageable? Would it have mitigated my "spa days"? Looking back, I see how victories could have been even more fulfilling, celebrated with those who rallied behind the same goals.

Acknowledging that this latest project stretched beyond my familiar terrain in technology, I recognized my need for guidance. My mantra became a wisdom-filled adage: "We are the company we keep." I set out to ally myself with those at the pinnacle of their fields, hoping their excellence and creativity would infuse our joint endeavors with boundless potential.

Fortune smiled upon me early on when I crossed paths with Aisha Marshall. To describe her as merely influential would be an understatement; Aisha has been the conductor of much of what I've accomplished. Even the essence of this chapter, speaking of a "cocoon season", metamorphosis, and transformation, is homage to Alisha and her perspective: *Butterfly SZN*. From our inaugural Zoom call, she exuded a sincerity and brilliance that stood apart from anyone I had met. Her warmth and wisdom flowed through our conversation, which unfolded with an unprecedented ease. Within the first 20 minutes — that first meaningful exchange — I felt an unfamiliar sense of safety. It rattled me, this break from my guarded norm, but the connection felt divinely orchestrated, compelling me to trust and surrender to the experience.

My gamble paid dividends. Aisha did not just meet my expectations; she surpassed them. Generously, she opened her formidable network, her sharp acumen lighting the way to success. Together we navigated formidable business challenges, but more importantly, she urged me to grow personally, pushing me beyond my comfort zones both within and outside the sphere of work. "Good company on a journey makes the way seem shorter," I owe Aisha an immeasurable debt, one that exceeds any expression of gratitude.

In sharing my narrative, I pay tribute not just to her expertise but to her role as a beacon of transformative change and growth. No words can sufficiently capture her monumental influence. Such recognition isn't about flattery — for her ego is uninvolved — but about acknowledging her indelible impact on the world around her.

This leads me to another lesson learned: the power of vulnerability. It might not come naturally, it might make you squirm, but heartfelt expression is vital. Those who have made a lasting impression, those who contribute positively to our lives, deserve to be recognized and commended. It's in these moments of transparent communication that we convey genuine appreciation, an acknowledgment often missing from daily experiences.

My third epiphany centers on trusting that inner voice. Follow the instincts that resonate at the core of your being. When an idea seems outlandishly ambitious, that's a cue to listen closer. It's a cue to take the plunge into the unknown.

If I'm faced with opportunities that push my boundaries, I now lean into the stretch. When my inner skeptic shouts in protest, I take it as a sign to definitely proceed. This approach may seem counterintuitive, but the results are invariably miraculous. By consistently challenging my past methods, I have witnessed an expansion across all facets of life — from business growth to personal wellness and enriched relationships.

Beneath all the lessons, the underlying "secret sauce" of my entire experience has been the unwavering love and encouragement of my partner. This solid and steadfast foundation has enabled me to revel in the triumphs, not alone but in partnership, and critically aided in weathering the trials.

Today success has shed its once grueling mantle to reveal a more balanced mix of challenge, satisfaction, and joy. My "spa days" now genuinely resemble respite and rejuvenation. In my interactions, I aspire to forge connections steeped in meaning rather than appearing purely transactional. Known for my tenacity in tackling complex issues, my goal has shifted from exploiting problems to harnessing opportunities for collective gain and heartfelt engagement.

This chapter of life's odyssey underscores the transformation that alignment, collaboration, vulnerability, and intuition can bring about. It's a testament to how the integration of shared knowledge, the willingness to expose one's soul, and the courage to heed gut feelings pave the way for astonishing growth and achievement. I now know that each season builds on the last, each cocooning ushers in a period of metamorphosis and transformation. With each season, I have been guided back to myself, transforming into the person I was always meant to be, safe to plunge into the unknown.

EMBRACING TRANSFORMATION AND GROWTH WITH PERSONAL INSIGHTS

This exercise, inspired by personal stories and insights, will help you navigate through your transformation journey. It emphasizes the importance of confronting discomfort, choosing greatness over complacency, valuing rest, and tuning into your intuition for authentic growth.

STEPS:

1. **EXPLORING THE UNCOMFORTABLE:**
    a. Action: Reflect on a situation where you felt discomfort or injustice. Identify a specific area in your life that you've avoided due to its discomfort.

b. Personal Insight: Drawing from my journey, consider how each encounter with discomfort strengthened my resilience and ultimately led to growth. Write down how confronting your discomfort could lead to your personal expansion.

2. **LETTING GO FOR GREATNESS:**
   a. Action: Identify an aspect of your life that's "good enough" but not fulfilling — similar to my realization that good should not be a barrier to great.
   b. Personal Insight: Inspired by my process of releasing what was merely good, write a commitment to yourself to pursue what feels authentically right and opens doors to greatness.

3. **BALANCING WORK WITH REST:**
   a. Action: Evaluate your lifestyle for imbalances between work and rest, inspired by my own "spa days of burnout". Plan meaningful rest activities.
   b. Personal Insight: Implement this balance for a month, and reflect in a journal. Note any shifts in well-being, paralleling my journey towards valuing rest as much as work itself.

4. **EMBRACING FLEXIBILITY AND INTUITION:**
   a. Action: Practice mindfulness to enhance your intuition, drawing inspiration from my advocacy for intuition over logic.
   b. Personal Insight: Weekly, document instances where intuition led you, and reflect on the

outcomes. Consider how being open and flexible, as I learned, supports your growth.

5. **ENGAGING WITH TRANSFORMATIONAL CONTENT:**
   a. Action: Dive into "Butterfly SZN: The Guided Journal," by Aishal Marshall, a source of inspiration and support for many. Allow it to bring significance to your life's transformative cycles, contextualize the seasons, and motivate your transformation journey.
   b. Personal Insight: Reflect on your seasons and capture the naturally inspired actions informed by your insights and understanding. Plan actionable steps to integrate these learnings into your daily life.

ABOUT
SABRINA STOROZUK

Sabrina Storozuk is an entrepreneur who has dedicated her career to technology transformations. She specializes in bringing outpaced industries up to speed with what is happening now in tech. From solutions services, to technology consulting at PWC, Sabrina has led transformations in both small ventures and large corporations.

Her new venture, ARC, is an intersection of her work in tech and her passion for women's health, specifically hair health. A headband that is as versatile as it is elegant, ARC is the first of its kind. Sabrina's journey with persistent gray roots led her to frequent salon visits, expensive treatments, and ultimately, trying every headband on the market. ARC is the tech transformation of the hair industry, allowing women to express their individuality and embrace their unique hair journeys with confidence, turning the simple act of wearing a headband into a transformative and liberating experience.

CHAPTER THREE
DON'T GO ALONE

RACHEL WOODWARD

IN BUSINESS AND LIFE, growth and expansion often require stepping out of your comfort zone. Taking a risk, overcoming a fear, having a difficult conversation, or challenging your own belief system. These moments are rarely comfortable and sometimes can seem unbearable, but it's when you finally emerge on the other side that you realize your true strength, capabilities, and that you can achieve things far beyond anything that you'd ever imagined.

Five years ago, I started dating Taylor; a stud of a man who is now my husband. When we met, he was living on a boat in Marina del Rey. Born and raised in Santa Monica, he grew up in the ocean and I still sometimes think he was misplaced as a human instead of a sea animal. He loves being in the ocean, swimming with whales and dolphins, and scuba diving to absurd depths. You name it, he'll swim with it.

This is a far contrast from me who was also born and raised in Southern California, but much prefers the beauty of *looking* at the ocean, rather than diving into it. Safely on the sand, I can appreciate the extremity of the ocean without needing to be in it. I was terrified of being in the ocean. So much so that I cried on a few of our "awesome" boating dates, ones where I wasn't even in the water.

For fun, Taylor was teaching freediving classes. I'd never heard of free diving but if it involved diving into the ocean, it was a hard 'no' for me. I often felt bad because he was so passionate about being in the water; I wished it was something I could share with him. I would listen to Taylor tell stories of how he got to give his students an experience that meant so much to him. I'd hear about the improvements the students would make throughout the weekend and how deep each one could dive by the end. He was so passionate, yet I still avoided the classes like a plague.

After about a year of freediving stories and watching his face light up while talking about his different classes, I decided to give it a go. His upcoming class was full of women which was rare and felt like a sign that it was my time to dive in, literally. We spent the Saturday on his boat, learning about our anatomy underwater and all the incredible ways that our bodies adjust to diving deep in the ocean under an enormous amount of pressure for an extended period of time. It was fascinating. It was also terrifying. We finished the day at the pool, learning proper diving techniques.

On Sunday, everyone arrived back at the boat. I was terrified and tried to hold back tears as we headed towards Catalina, one the many small islands off the coast of California. We boated out about ten miles and then stopped. The girls and I suited up while Taylor got the floating devices situated. I looked around at the other women, then glanced at Taylor and thought to myself, "I'm not going. I'll lay on the boat and tan." Then my gut turned, reminding me that I was capable. I signed up for the class to experience something new and I couldn't chicken out now. I jumped off the boat and into the cold water.

That day, I dove over 50 feet deep into the ocean. I felt the pressure build against my body the further down I went. I was shocked at how much the temperature would drop the further down I went. I saw the colors surrounding me change from dark and eerie to even darker and eerier. I felt all these intense sensations while at the same time needing to remain calm to preserve the oxygen I needed to get back to the surface. It was terrifying. But I did it. I couldn't believe I did it, and truthfully, I still can't.

That day, in one of the most intimidating ways possible, I experienced the same ocean that had crippled me with fear for my entire life. To see it in a new perspective was exhilarating and eye opening.

Over the next few days, I was on a high. I thought to myself, "If I could get through the freediving class and feel this good, what else is possible?" I also started to think about the stories I would tell myself and the profound impact my words had on how I was living my life. False narratives of fear that I had built up like a shield, suddenly began to crumble. I noticed that the way I was speaking to myself was not conducive to growth and that it was holding me back from not jus epic personal experiences, but also growth in all areas of my life, including business.

How was my mindset affecting my business? What about my relationships? I was surprised at how a small and temporary shift in perspective could give me the courage to do something

I wouldn't normally do. What if I opened my mind to other experiences that I was previously closed to? How much more *life* would I get to experience?

I have experienced other, perspective-shifting moments in my life as a businesswoman, a wife, daughter, friend, and a human being who is always seeking opportunities for growth and expansion. Some of these moments, like my free dive, may seem insignificant in the grand scheme of life but can ultimately be a massive catalyst for growth.

By taking a plunge into the unknown and by being open to experiencing discomfort in exchange for growth, we can recognize our true potential, make deeper and more meaningful connections, and live a more vibrant life.

Not long after my freediving experience, I was setting goals for the new year, including goals for my business. My broad goal was growth, and I knew that to take my business to the next level, I needed to increase my visibility. I've always preferred working behind the scenes or one on one with clients. I've never been big on self-promotion or on discussing my success in business. I wasn't sure what becoming more visible meant at the time, I just had a feeling that visibility was what I needed.

Not long after that conversation with myself, I was scrolling through Instagram and saw a post about a free masterclass on how to become more visible, credible, and profitable. I'd never joined a masterclass before but how could I say no? It was just what I needed.

The next day I logged on and there was a lot of pink and feminine energy. It was different, but I was open. That week, I showed up every day at 9 am. Always uncomfortable but eager to hear more. I participated in the awkward warm up dance, even with my camera on. I shared out loud with the group and in the chat. I spoke about my goals and even about my insecurities. I was engaged in a way that felt incredibly uncomfortable but also like I was exactly where I needed to be.

After dipping my toes in the water, I spent the next six months with this same group of women discussing business, strategy, and inevitably, how the heck to be more visible. With some guidance and a loving push in the right direction, I slowly started to share my knowledge, expertise in my business, and client successes. I applied to, and have been featured on, multiple podcasts that discuss the financial side of healthcare. And to my surprise those podcasts have earned me three new clients! I've hosted webinars, written numerous articles, and most reluctantly began speaking about my professional life on social media.

As I began to share my professional journey and expertise with others, I witnessed a profound shift in my business, my perspective, and most surprisingly in my personal relationships. By throwing myself into the uncomfortable unknown, I discovered new, meaningful relationships with individuals that I may have otherwise never crossed paths with; I felt supported and understood by my new friends in an exciting and uniquely special way. It was the beginning of a major transformation. Sure, visibility was the goal, and it was working, but the growth I experienced on the other side of that was the real prize.

My biggest fear in my "visibility journey" was, surprisingly, being judged by my friends and family. Would they think I was taking myself too seriously or question my newly expressive enthusiasm for my career? Would I be seen as narcissistic? These thoughts felt paralyzing. However, by throwing those stories out the window and facing my own insecurities head on, I have not only created more opportunities for myself in business, but deeper and more meaningful connections with those closest to me.

Many of the people who I was irrationally afraid would judge me have shown interest in what I am doing and have even told me that I've motivated them to start something that they'd been thinking about. Acquaintances have connected me to potential clients and my network has grown in an organic and meaningful way. By putting myself out there, I learned that many people are more willing to take the plunge than I initially assumed, and it feels good to bring them along for the ride!

Perhaps my biggest challenge to date is continuing to step into thought leadership in my industry. It is far from my comfort zone but ultimately, I know it will bring me exponential growth, both personally and professionally. I have always prided myself on my operational skills: my ability to see problems from a wide lens and then develop tactile solutions to solve them. I love an organized spreadsheet, refined systems and processes, and meeting with my team members on a regular basis to discuss strategy and workflow. My memory for fine and sometimes irrelevant details is sharp and I take great pleasure in working behind the scenes.

As you'd probably guess, public speaking and hosting live webinars aren't on the top of my list. In fact, I have a similar reaction to public speaking as I once did to freediving: *hard no*. Just the words 'public speaking' themselves make me uncomfortable. The act of physically doing it? Absolutely not an experience I would normally seek out on my own. But as life has shown me time and time again, the more uncomfortable I get, the greater the reward is on the other side.

As a result, I decided to host my first webinar. I sent the invite to the 300 people on our company's email list. Consisting of current and former clients, warm and cold leads, acquaintances that I'd met at webinars and anyone who'd previously subscribed to our company blog. I posted about the webinar on my personal and company LinkedIn profile and reached out to clients directly to extend the invitation.

Much to my surprise, the reaction was quite positive. Over 30 people signed up within the first few days, but not just two: two health care facilities we work with told me that they were going to have their entire clinical staff sit in on the webinar. To me, this was a double edged sword; I obviously wanted the webinar to be a success, but the *fear* of stepping into the spotlight was exorbitant.

The subject of the webinar, "How to Chart for Insurance Authorization & Audits" is a topic that I am very familiar with. I've gone through this framework hundreds of times with my team, behavioral health attorneys, facility owners and clinicians, and insurance auditors. I know this subject like the back of my hand. However, just as I hesitated to step off the boat in the freediving class, my fear of the spotlight, even if it was only 30 people, felt daunting.

For a long time, there has been a voice in my head encouraging me to share the things that are important to me. Be it work, where I help countless individuals get access to healthcare by managing the insurance revenue cycle, or my passion for fitness and movement. I've dismissed my urges to share publicly for fear of judgment, imperfection, or not living up to my own, very high standard.

But at some point, enough is enough. You just have to jump.

For the record, sharing about my career in a public way is still very uncomfortable, but when we move into a space of discomfort, we are physically changing and strengthening our brain's neuroplasticity which allows us to better adapt and respond to life's stressors.

Even as a successful, confident woman, I regularly face self-doubt and fear of criticism from others. Great days and big wins are sometimes followed by new obstacles and setbacks. However, by remaining resilient and staying true to my vision, I know I can overcome these challenges and continue to progress forward. It's when we learn to view fear as a catalyst for growth rather than a hindrance, that we begin embracing discomfort as a more welcomed challenge.

Below, I've outlined a few strategies that can help you move *out* of fear and *into* expansion.

1. CULTIVATE A GROWTH MINDSET: View challenges as opportunities. When you feel like you are in the weeds, take a moment to visualize or journal about what is waiting for you on the other side.
2. SET GOALS: Establishing clear goals provides direction and motivation to keep going, especially in moments of doubt or insecurity.
3. PRACTICE SELF-COMPASSION: Be kind to yourself as you would to your best friend, recognizing that growth takes time.

4. SEEK SUPPORT: Surround yourself with a supportive network – people who can provide guidance and encouragement.
5. TAKE INCREMENTAL STEPS: Break larger goals into smaller, manageable tasks
6. REFLECT: Take time to reflect on your experiences, identifying lessons learned and areas for growth.

The journey of embracing discomfort is an ongoing process—one that requires courage, resilience, and a willingness to step into the unknown. Whether it's taking a freediving class, increasing visibility, pursuing a new opportunity, or facing personal challenges with a new perspective, taking the plunge is essential for transformation.

We must embrace fear and discomfort as a catalyst for change, and recognize that on the other side lies endless possibility and opportunity for ultimate fulfillment. So, I encourage you to:

1. FIND YOUR TRIBE: Those who support and uplift you, and who believe in you before you are sure for yourself.
2. LEAN INTO YOUR FEARS AND EMBRACE VULNERABILITY. Take risks and trust in your ability to conquer challenges. It's okay to be fearful but *never* let fear hold you back.

ABOUT
RACHEL WOODWARD

This chapter is dedicated to my Mama, my rock and biggest supporter & to the inspirational women of The Pitch Club Inner Circle - thank you for encouraging me to step out of my comfort zone.

Rachel Woodward is a healthcare advocate, bestselling author, and the CEO of Datapro Billing Service. As an expert in insurance reimbursement, Rachel helps health care providers and facilities optimize and project their finances and manage insurance billing so that they are able focus on high quality care while maintaining confidence in their bottom line.

Her expertise has been featured on leading podcasts such as Perspectives in Health Care with Rob Oliver, Behind The Scenes with Sonda, The Practice of The Practice, and more.

CHAPTER FOUR
MISS-UNDERSTOOD

HARLEY JORDAN

RECENTLY, I WAS LET IN ON A LITTLE SECRET. The moments that stick with you, the ones that glow in your mind and can be recalled in an instant like your favorite catchy lyrics, are the ones that will continue popping up most frequently throughout the rest of your life. Think about it: the light hitting their face just so, their words sparking something permanent in your chest, the background blurring as if your memory switches to portrait mode. This glow is not happenstance; it's a little bookmark from the universe, a reminder for the times you're meant to carry with you, always.

There's magic in these moments because you are meant to learn from them. Even in the moments that don't glow, but burn.

A giggle I was meant to learn from took place in a sunny college basketball gym in the middle of January. The stuffy smell of old roll-up cheerleading mats filled the air almost as strongly as the perpetual chant of "ONE, THREE, FIVE, SEVEN," as we kept pace with the music.

My coach was a Texas transplant living in southern California. He held more championship titles than years I had been alive and had the attitude to prove it. This particular practice, he stopped us as yet another cheerleader face planted on the mat, which up close was an artistic vision of years of smeared foundation, mascara, sweat, and who knows what else.

"None of you are going anywhere! You can't even pull it together for a simple task! You will never do anything important with your lives!" He bellowed.

I let out a giggle, scanning the room only to find a sea of serious faces staring at their feet. Oops! Quick switcheroo to serious mode. There I was, 19 and bursting at the seams with grand plans, a non-coffee drinker with energy levels that could rival a caffeinated squirrel. His "going nowhere" jab? Yeah, it was clear as day that box wasn't built for me. I had a one-way ticket to Big Deal Station, and no amount of grumpy side-eye was about to derail this train.

So, I discarded it, all the while unknowingly constructing a metaphorical box for myself:

Hard work beats talent when talent doesn't work hard.

Months later, I scampered over to the hairsprayed and self tanned group circling outside the Anaheim Convention Center, smoothie in hand.

My coach glanced up at me, frowning, "You all should be looking at Harley."

My immensely talented team turned to my unsuspecting face.

I squared my shoulders, ready for the jab I knew was speeding my way. Late by ten whole seconds? Check. Sauntering at snail-speed when I should apparently be plowing through the crowd like a bulldozer? Guilty as charged. The scolding for my ever-so-slight tardiness was as predictable as a rerun of my favorite sitcom. And there it came — the call-out, right on cue. Just another day in the life of an ever so charming slow walker.

"She puts in the work and extra hours. Hard work beats talent when talent doesn't work hard. She isn't the most talented but she looks better than any of you out there!" My coach berated the group.

"The rest of you have rested on your talent this season!"

I didn't know whether to be proud or insulted. As if it were a carnival funhouse, my not-quite-done-developing prefrontal cortex distorted each snarky remark. Deciphering how to file the comment into long term memory.

Ah, the joys of a teenage brain!

'So, he thinks I'm short on talent?' I thought to myself.

'Makes sense that he's never made an effort to actually coach me this season. No talent equals not worth his precious time.' my thoughts began to spiral.

'But wait — this isn't the finale of my life's melodramatic plotline. I've got a work ethic that would shame a workhorse. There's a teeny-tiny glimmer of hope if I just hustle harder. I could sneak past success's bouncers.'

'So what if no one's betting on my talent? I'll give him a plot twist. I'll work my butt off to camouflage this so-called

deficiency. Talent, schmalent. I'm making this work, one overachievement at a time.'

Let me be perfectly clear: I was competing at the highest level of cheerleading in an international, co-ed division. We used to pile out of the car at busy stop lights and do back tucks on concrete for fun. It's laughable to imply that this 19 year old athlete was untalented.

So there I was, embracing the Hard Work Box like it was going out of style. I strutted through college, credits shooting passed the graduation requirement like I was trying to beat a high score in an arcade game. 'Overtime' became my middle name. Self-care? Ha, why focus on my own needs when I can just hide them under shiny badges and success.

Before I was 22 years old, my resume included managing 20+ employees, training professional basketball players in agility, and a nutrition certification I've never used. Talent was one thing, but boy, did I have hustle.

Then came the pandemic, and not even that could strip me of my beloved Badge of Busy. A month into lockdown, and I felt the heaviness of those words I had been trying to outrun crash into me: hard work beats talent when talent doesn't work hard. I might have been jobless during the onset of The Pandemic, but I wouldn't be motionless. So, what did I do? I leapt into my biggest undertaking yet.

I began to carve out the career I once thought required a few more birthdays, a more sensible wardrobe, and an extra dash of professionalism. And it all kicked off with a post on Instagram. Who knew? My ticket to the big leagues wouldn't come from crunching numbers in a suit clad board room but hamming it up in my kitchen for seven second videos I would post on Instagram. Yet, underneath the digital applause, I spiraled. Did I need to be less blonde, less bubby, and reverse my nonexistent interest in corporate hierarchy to hit the big time?

The thought of being tagged as an "Influencer" sent shivers down my spine. In my head, "influencer" equaled easy street: talent and privilege taking the front seat while hard work got booted to the back. No way did that title scream "hardest worker in the room."

To the outside eye, Influencers are the ultimate cool girls, right? Society's got us thinking they're all about that easy life: lounging by pools, peddling diet shakes at the cost of their morals. Glued to their phones, not because they crave genuine connection, but because it's all about racking up the likes and living a selfie-centric lifestyle.

No.

Influencers are drawn to the internet because they don't have the same understanding and acceptance in their real world.

They aren't the cool girls; so they pretend.

They fake it.

They work hard.

Because hard work beats talent when talent doesn't work hard.

And women work hard.

If Influencer marketing was a male dominated industry, it would be called business and influencers would be called entrepreneurs. The feminine ability to connect with people across the world by sharing their inner musings would be seen as the amazing skill that it is. Influence only comes from true connection and true connection comes from shared feelings.

The best way to be influential is to say it with your chest.

As my followers grew, so did my unease with what I was somewhat accidentally building. And then, in a scene worthy of a corny sound effect, I got hit with the exact question I'd dreaded: "So, what do you do?"

Brain freeze. Full system error. Sure, I could've easily said I was a coach — I mean, I *was* a coach. But nope, out came the word I dreaded most:

Influencer.

Just like that, I flung myself into the very box I'd been tiptoeing around.

To my utter shock, the person across from me didn't miss a beat.

"You're not just an influencer. I've seen your posts. You're building something big," they chimed in, their voice cutting through the surrounding chatter as my brain switched to portrait mode, etching a moment into memory.

I did my best to control my glow of pride but I felt like a human disco ball.

I had done it. My meticulously chosen words and captions weren't just for fun; they were a carefully constructed facade for an "eternally hustling" persona. And despite my slip-up, my cover remained unblown. My "lack of talent" was buried deep like cursed treasure. And I wanted this dark secret to be buried so deep it would need its own map. Like a spy with a blown cover, "lack of talent" was going dark.

I wasn't just making waves; I was the storm. Helping thousands, building an online community that would fill two basketball arenas, launching a podcast, and on a wild impulse, creating an Influencer Talent Agency from scratch.

Who's untalented now?

If you've ever gotten caught in 'just watch me' energy, you know the feeling. The masochism sinks in as another opportunity to prove yourself hits you in the gut. Realistically, I didn't want an agency but more than that, I didn't want the responsibility of picking my next label. If I picked, there was a chance it wouldn't be universally accepted. I latched onto 'Agency Owner' because it seemed to radiate universal success even though it felt like perpetual frustration.

I hit rock bottom trying to keep up this facade. Most days, my brain felt like an overheating laptop trying to keep up with 754 unread emails, 46 missed texts, and approximately 311 open tabs. In fact, this is the current status of my iPhone. Now a coffee addict, I drank far too much in a frantic attempt to keep up with my To Do List. I developed stress ulcers. I stopped working out. I felt the weight of the world.

Meanwhile, Agency finances painted a brighter picture. We could sell to the highest bidder in a matter of years.

Spoiler alert: we didn't sell to the highest bidder.

I felt the light draining from me. The girl that just a few years prior was worried she had to become less blonde, less bubby, and reverse her nonexistent interest in corporate hierarchy slowly became less blonde, less bubby, and really wished she had someone to toss the baton to.

Diving headfirst into the unknown usually screams bravery, right? Like nailing that speech, throwing cash into the next big endeavor, or piecing together your dream venture. For me, bravery had a different flavor. It was about cozying up to the idea that in putting my own needs first, I might just ruffle some feathers — be it my team, my community, my family, or anyone who ever thought my job title was the coolest thing since sliced bread.

What if they think there's bad blood? What if they think I don't care? What if they think it flopped? What if they think this is a mistake? My thoughts spiraled for weeks.

On November 9th, 2023, it hit me smack in the face that it was time to walk away.

I wrote this my notes:

Tell business partner

Tell employees

Tell clients

Launch a new podcast to share my feelings

Suddenly, I was in full-on release mode: letting go of the grand plan, ditching the deadlines, and tossing aside the old box I'd been trying to fit into.

With no open ended worries that I might miss something important, I closed every lingering tab in my brain.

This story is not about a big business failure nor a backhanded compliment from a bitter old man. It's about letting someone else control the labels you hold. I sure as hell didn't lack talent. I was lonely and tired of not fitting in with the "cool girls." My Badge of Busy was a distraction. If I slowed down, I would have to face my own feelings and risk choosing my own labels.

I felt misunderstood.

But there's something special about feelings. There's only so many. You might be a unique, beautiful snowflake with a wonderful, impactful story to share but you are not the only one experiencing the specific jumble of thoughts, feelings, and fears that are spiraling around your big, intelligent brain.

Being misunderstood is a myth we use to keep our masks on and avoid actually sharing.

So, I dove right in, bid adieu to my cherished Badge of Busy, and confronted the question head-on:

What if I could just be me, without feeling the need to convince anyone of anything?

What if I am inherently…

Influential

Impactful

Talented

Intelligent

Enough

Understood

A big deal

We don't micromanage our hearts to keep them pumping, nor do we micromanage our blood to keep it flowing. Maybe the best approach is to stop the tug-of-war with perception and simply choose to be.

I chose not to put myself in the "going nowhere" box and therefore, I went somewhere. Alternatively, I actively chose to put myself in the "hardworking business owner" box.

So no, you don't have to try with all your might to ensure you don't come off as:

Lazy
A know it all
Inconsiderate
Dumb
Aggressive
Ignorant
Too young to get it
Too busy to care
Mean
Lame
Annoying
Loner

Insert the word that stings the most.

Simply choose.

Society often paints the picture that big bold success hinges on staying one step ahead of the world. We're led to believe we need to be first or else we are last. We need to say it best or else we are irrelevant.

On social media, this means frantically pouring every ounce of our intellect into snagging a scroller's fleeting attention. We clear the laundry explosion from our background and arrange our hair to look just relatable enough. We hope that our work day looks aspirational while packing captions with every bit of information possible.

Do more. Be more.

I cannot get behind this.

We are not here to teach, we are here to share.

Share your experience.

Share your feelings.

Share your biggest struggles.

Because your biggest struggles will create the biggest impact.

So to my 19 year old self I say:

You are an ever evolving person in an ever changing world. You have the power to change, to grow, to evolve. But as you embark on this journey of growth and evolution, always remember: you're the one calling the shots.

You are influential without faking it. You are intelligent regardless of mistakes. You are not alone even when you feel misunderstood. If you worry about coming off as too loud, too annoying, too aggressive, remember, *you choose*.

Say it with your chest!

I am a hardworking, talented, and ethical influencer. Period. No debates, no negotiations. How do I know? Because I choose to be.

ABOUT
HARLEY JORDAN

Harley Jordan is a seasoned social media strategist, renowned host of "Not Your Mother's Influencer Podcast," and the founder of an influencer talent agency. With a passion for empowering women, Harley specializes in guiding wise women to show up big and share their story through her disruptive "Do Less" process.

CHAPTER FIVE

THE DIVE INTO DESTINY: NAVIGATING THE WATERS OF CHANGE

PAIGE DUNGAN

IN MY JOURNEY, THERE CAME A MOMENT, a pivotal turning point that felt as though the horizon itself was unfolding before me. It wasn't the familiar, comforting continuity of a path I had long traversed, but rather a daring leap into depths unknown. This moment whispered of liberation, a beckoning into realms untamed and unexplored, far from the rigid boundaries that had once hemmed me in. This chapter of my life wasn't just about stepping off the beaten path; it was an invitation to cast aside the heavy yoke of societal norms and the weighty expectations that had tethered my spirit to the docks of conformity.

I found myself embracing the exhilarating uncertainty that comes with charting my own course, guided only by the steadfast beacon of my inner truth. Here, in these open waters, I summoned the courage to navigate by my own stars, to steer by the light of my deepest values and dreams. This voyage demanded boldness to face the tempests of doubt and the gales of fear.

Yet, it was amidst this tumult that I discovered the essence of my being, an unshakeable conviction in my ability to forge a destiny that resonates with the core of who I am.

THE ILLUSION OF LIGHT

For a long time, I rode the high of what I believed was my personal spotlight. My life seemed to be lifted straight from a glossy magazine, ticking off the boxes for what society labeled as "success." A career that had me jet-setting, rubbing shoulders with the glamorous, and soaking in applause — it all felt like I was living the dream. I was molded, willingly, by expectations that weren't entirely my own but were dazzling enough to make me overlook any inner voice saying, *'but wait, is this me?'* Success, as it was defined by the world around me, seemed to fit just right, and I embraced it with open arms.

But life has a funny way of throwing curveballs.

Standing on the brink of motherhood for the second time, something shifted. The light that once seemed so brilliant began to waver. It was as if someone had flipped a switch, and the glow that surrounded me started to show its true colors. What was once a beacon of achievement began to look more like a glaring spotlight, highlighting the facade rather than the reality. The glamour and the constant chase that had once fueled my days no longer seemed fulfilling. It was like waking up from a dream and realizing that the storyline wasn't quite what you thought it was.

This flickering light wasn't just a sign of change; it was a wake-up call. It made me question everything I had been striving for.

Was chasing this predefined notion of success really worth it?

The roles I played, the accolades I chased; did they truly resonate with the person I wanted to be?

Suddenly, the career that once seemed to define success felt more like a golden cage, one that I had willingly entered.

The realization was startling but necessary. It wasn't just about stepping out of the spotlight; it was about turning off the switch entirely and finding my own light. One that illuminated a path defined not by societal benchmarks but by what truly mattered to me. Motherhood, with all its challenges and joys, offered a lens through which I could reassess my priorities and redefine success on my own terms.

This journey wasn't about abandoning ambition but redirecting it towards what genuinely fulfilled me. It was a call to forge a path where success wasn't measured by fame or accolades but by happiness, contentment, and the legacy I would leave for my children. The flickering light turned out to be the beacon I needed, guiding me towards a life that felt authentic and true to who I am.

THE FIRST PLAN-LESS STEP

My meticulously crafted life, designed to balance societal acceptance with personal ambition, had always felt secure. Yet, it was the upheaval following the birth of my second child that shattered this illusion of control.

Postpartum anxiety gripped me with a ferocity I hadn't anticipated, challenging every aspect of my identity and the life I had built. This profound crisis, somehow manifested itself in an unexpected clarity and became the catalyst for a seismic shift in my perspective. Without a safety net, I stepped off the life-tightrope I had been walking, propelled by a mix of fear, hope, and an indescribable sense of freedom.

At 35, responsible for two young, impressionable lives, and standing within the walls of a home that whispered promises of new beginnings, I confronted the reality of my existence.

The fortress of achievement and expectation I had constructed around me began to crumble, revealing its fragile foundation.

My struggle with postpartum anxiety was not just a battle to regain my sense of self; it was a wake-up call to reassess what truly mattered. The voices that had once urged me to maintain the status quo now seemed distant. The allure of a life, unscripted and genuine, became impossible to ignore.

Embracing this vulnerability, I chose to pivot away from the path others had laid out for me. This wasn't an act of rebellion but a deliberate step toward authenticity. The journey through postpartum anxiety had exposed the cracks in my carefully curated life, urging me to seek fulfillment beyond societal accolades and superficial success.

It was in this turbulent period of self-discovery that the seeds of entrepreneurship were sown. My decision to forge a new path was not merely about distancing myself from a predefined career trajectory; it was about channeling my experiences, my struggles, and my victories into something transformative.

Starting my own business became an extension of my journey towards healing and self-realization. *It was a venture born out of necessity. A way to rebuild my identity and assert control over my narrative.*

Entrepreneurship offered me a platform to harness the insights gained from my battle with postpartum anxiety and to create a venture that was not only a reflection of my values but also a testament to the resilience of the human spirit. In building my business, I found a unique opportunity to advocate for issues close to my heart, including mental health awareness and support for parents navigating similar challenges.

This transition into entrepreneurship was more than a career shift; it was a vital step in my recovery and growth. It symbolized a break from the past, a reclamation of agency, and a commitment to living a life that was not only successful by my own standards but also rich with purpose and meaning. Through this journey, I discovered that true fulfillment comes not from external validation but from the courage to pursue one's passions and to live authentically, even in the face of uncertainty and adversity.

THE LEGACY I CHOOSE

My entrepreneurship journey, from its conception, has been a testament to resilience, discovery, and the courage to embrace change. The initial leap into starting an agency with my incredible co-founder was fueled by passion and a drive to create something meaningful. As we navigated the complex landscape of building a business, our strengths and opportunities grew, but so did the realization that our paths were diverging. Facing a significant turning point, we made the difficult decision to go our separate ways, each of us turning down a different road.

This pivotal moment, occurring within the first tumultuous year of business together, brought me to the brink of giving up. However, through a profound process of self-reflection, I found clarity and reassurance in my purpose, realizing I was exactly where I was meant to be.

The decision to split up the agency was both an ending and a beginning.

A year into this incredible journey, I was faced with the challenge of starting over, this time on my own. The transition from partnership to solo entrepreneur wasn't just about restructuring a business; it was about redefining my identity as an entrepreneur. The lessons learned from the past, the successes, the failures, and most importantly, the growth, became the foundation upon which I built my new venture.

This new chapter wasn't just a continuation of my entrepreneurial story; it was a rebirth, marked by a deeper understanding of my own capabilities and a clearer vision for the future. Starting anew, I leaned into the insights gained from my experiences, using them to shape the direction and values of my new business. This solo venture allowed me to fully embrace the lessons learned from my struggles with postpartum anxiety, the dissolution of a partnership, and the daunting yet exhilarating challenge of building something from scratch.

The journey of restarting my business alone was a profound exercise in self-trust and determination. It taught me that entrepreneurship is not just about the business you build but the person you become in the process. Every setback, every challenge, and every moment of doubt was an opportunity for growth, pushing me to become a more resilient, insightful, and compassionate leader.

Now, as I reflect on the path that led me here, I see a story of transformation. My entrepreneurship journey—from the excitement of the initial launch with a co-founder to the challenges of going solo—has been a journey of constant learning and adaptation. It's a narrative that underscores the importance of perseverance, the value of self-reflection, and the power of starting over with a renewed sense of purpose. This journey has

THE DIVE INTO DESTINY: NAVIGATING THE WATERS OF CHANGE

not only shaped my business but has fundamentally transformed me, illustrating that with every challenge comes an opportunity to learn, grow, and move closer to where you're truly meant to be.

FAN THE FLAMES, SET SAIL, STEP INTO THE SUN

Embarking on a journey to reshape my life and career, I learned something vital: *transformation is not just a goal, it's a continuous process*. I started with a small spark of desire for something different, something more authentic to who I am. By embracing change and daring to dream, I've launched not just a new agency but another business as well, each a reflection of my once-silenced voice now fully expressed.

"Fan the Flames, Set Sail, Step into the Sun" has become my mantra, symbolizing my journey from reigniting my inner spark, to navigating changes, to shining in my true potential.

Almost three years into this adventure, I've realized I'm still very much a work in progress. Balancing my mental health with the demands of entrepreneurship is challenging. The mix isn't always perfect, and there are days when doubts and stresses cloud the vision of what I'm building. Yet, it's precisely in these moments that the value of community becomes crystal clear.

Finding a community of like-minded individuals, who are navigating their own entrepreneurial journeys, has been a game-changer. They've become a source of support, understanding, and shared wisdom that's invaluable. This network has reminded me that while entrepreneurship is a path I walk independently, I don't have to do it in isolation.

As I continue to grow my businesses and myself, I'm learning that success isn't just about hitting targets or making waves. It's also about how well you can maintain your well-being, lean on and contribute to your community, and keep fanning the flames of your ambition, even on the tough days. My journey is far from over, but with every step, I'm finding more of my voice, my strength, and my place in a community that lifts me up.

GROWING WITH INTENTION

During a period where the ground beneath me seemed to shift constantly—ranging from upheavals in my personal life to unpredictable changes in my business and evolving dynamics in friendships, the "Circle of Control" exercise emerged as a beacon of clarity and empowerment. The process of distinguishing between what was within my grasp and what lay beyond my influence was transformative, grounding me in a time of turmoil.

THE CIRCLE OF CONTROL: MY ANCHOR IN THE STORM

STEP 1: DRAW TWO CIRCLES, ONE INSIDE THE OTHER

Why It Matters: This visual representation embodies the fundamental principle that while we cannot control every aspect of our lives, there's always a part that remains under our influence. The act of drawing these circles serves as a physical manifestation of this concept, setting the stage for a deeper exploration of our internal and external worlds.

STEP 2: IDENTIFY & WRITE

Digging Deeper: This step invites a moment of introspection, urging us to distinguish between the external forces that shape our environment and the internal power we hold within ourselves.

By listing elements beyond our control in the outer circle (such as global events, others' actions, or societal expectations), we acknowledge their impact without allowing them to dictate our feelings or actions. Conversely, by identifying what we can control in the inner circle (our reactions, decisions, and mindset), we empower ourselves to take responsibility for our part in any situation.

Why It Matters: This distinction helps reduce feelings of helplessness or stress caused by focusing too much on uncontrollable factors. It shifts our focus to where we can make a real difference, fostering a sense of empowerment.

STEP 3: HIGHLIGHT & PLAN

Going Beyond Identification: Highlighting the most critical items within our control emphasizes our priorities and values. It's not enough to recognize what we can control; we must also decide how to act upon it. This step transforms awareness into action by requiring us to devise specific, tangible actions for each highlighted item.

Why It Matters: Planning actionable steps translates abstract concepts into concrete actions, making it easier to integrate these changes into our daily lives. It turns intention into practice.

STEP 4: COMMIT TO ACTION

Making It Real: Choosing one action and setting a reminder solidifies our commitment to ourselves. This step is about accountability, ensuring that our insights and plans don't remain on paper but become part of our lived experience.

Why It Matters: Commitment and follow-through are what set the stage for real change. By taking even a small step, we reinforce our agency and ability to influence our lives positively.

INTEGRATING THE EXERCISE INTO YOUR LIFE

Consistency is Key: Making this exercise a regular part of your routine — whether weekly, monthly, or during times of particular stress — can significantly impact your mindset and overall well-being. It serves as a recurring checkpoint, realigning your focus and actions with what truly matters to you.

Reflection and Growth: Over time, you might find that the items in your circles change, reflecting your growth, shifting priorities, or new challenges. This evolution is a natural part of the journey, offering insights into your personal development and the changing landscape of your life.

Sharing and Expanding: Consider sharing this exercise with friends, family, or colleagues. Discussing your circles can provide new perspectives, deepen your understanding, and foster a supportive community where growth and accountability are shared values.

By regularly engaging with the "Circle of Control" exercise, you're not merely navigating through life's challenges, you're actively shaping your path with intention, resilience, and a clear focus on what truly lies within your power to change. Here's to the unwritten chapters and the stories we continue to craft, one action at a time.

ABOUT
PAIGE DUNGAN

Paige Dungan is a highly regarded figure in the publishing world, known for her exceptional skills as a creative publicist. With a proven track record, she stands as the mastermind behind numerous triumphant book launches, garnering accolades for her role in catapulting multiple authors on best-seller lists. Before establishing her industry-leading book public relations agency, The Front Porch Collective, and publishing house 10/10 Press, Paige was the Head of PR & Talent at SUCCESS magazine. It was during her tenure at SUCCESS magazine that she embarked on her career in author and book campaigns. With more than 15 years of industry expertise, Paige has emerged as the ultimate resource for individuals aspiring to enter the realm of publishing and bring their dreams to fruition.

CHAPTER SIX
FROM SKYDIVE TO SAFETY NET

MELISSA DEAN

I'M THE KIND OF PERSON THAT LOVES the excitement of adventure and a leap of faith. Do you want to ride camels into the Sahara and sleep under the stars? Or hot air ballooning over the desert and then snorkel among sunken ships in the Red Sea? Sign me up!

Are you a person who loves to step up and take a leap? I think I can, with confidence, say that I am a "take a leap" kind of girl. I love new ideas, new beginnings, and the thrill of planning a new endeavor. I even decided to take my son skydiving to celebrate his 18th birthday.

As I have gotten a bit older and wiser, I've grown to realize that the floating (or sometimes falling) stage can be much more difficult for me than the initial plunge or leap itself. The last moment before freefall, the last tiny steps as you inch your way closer and closer to the door, preparing to jump out into the clear blue sky, can be terrifying; the preparation to open the doors on a new project, too, can feel like vertigo. "Is this really going to work?" or, "Did I plan enough, get the right people in my corner, think of every detail to avoid failure?"

I've changed, it seems. After years of being the person who inches with excitement towards the door of the plane, trusting that the guy I'm jumping with has it all worked out and that our parachute will open just as it's supposed to, I'm now someone who needs to know all the details of how to land us safely, long before we ever get near the door. Having a family, running a business, and supporting other families bring their family to life has changed me; I have brought others along with me in my journey and there are several of us together under that same parachute now. I am no longer the fearless jumper, in many ways I'm the safety net for others.

My name is Melissa Dean, and I am a homebirth midwife and functional medicine practitioner. I am the founder of Casa Natal Birth and Wellness Center. I am an expert in holistic women's health and in caring for women through pregnancy, birth, and in the months and years after giving birth. I say I chose midwifery, but I think it really chose me. Yes, I made the decision to go to school and study midwifery. But, it was only after my own birth experiences and then witnessing birth in the hospital — where the care for women was truly lacking — that I felt I needed to pursue that calling.

To feel safe and really seen is very unique in health care, but it changes a woman's experience from one of fear to an experience of strength. Traditional medicine practices and hospitals don't always provide this level of care. When a woman does not feel well or like themselves, they seek out medical care from their doctor. So often, however, they are dismissed, patronized or ignored. Being told, "oh that's just because you're a mother," or made to feel it's all in their head.

Many concerns and ailments that women have go unnoticed; it's statistically proven that women need to seek out care seven to nine times before they receive a proper diagnosis for thyroid issues, autoimmunity and GI disorders. These symptoms are then often treated with over-medication and lack proper attention.

By contrast, when women come into care with my practice, they are listened to, seen as a whole person with varying symptoms, and educated about the options that are available to them for their individual needs.

While seemingly subtle, offering personalized care can make a world of difference, not just in the treatment of a disease or illness, but also in the relationship between patient and provider. Witnessing this process is a gift I get to receive over and over again as I walk beside each of my clients through their birth, and then alongside them in the weeks afterward. I am their safety net as they take the plunge into motherhood. Encouraging them and sharing the joy as they grow in confidence and learn to trust their intuitions as mothers.

My care extends long past delivery: I help women regain health after years of feeling depleted, anxious, overwhelmed and ignored by other medical professionals. I help them get to the root of their health issues and then build a care program centered on what they need. After all, to be the best we can be as women and mothers we need to feel healthy and well!

When embarking on a career as a midwife, I saw a deep need for autonomy and informed consent. I became passionate about filling this gap in health care, and offering women options and safety when it came to their birth story. When I decided to become a midwife, I was raising my own four children and wanted to help others receive the holistic and natural birth experience that I had missed out on.

Soon after obtaining my license as a midwife, I opened a birth center to create an experience for those women who weren't quite ready for a home birth, but definitely didn't want to go to a hospital. I saw the need in my community and was eager to fill it. But, as I edged closer to the opening day, I knew the increasing overhead costs would require me to work just a bit more to make ends meet.

The eternal entrepreneur dilemma is this: Will I succeed? Do I have what it takes? Can I keep up with the new demands created from owning this business? Supporting a woman bringing new life into the world is one thing, but bringing a new business into the world is a whole new ballgame. I kept my overhead low and those first several years the practice grew slowly and began to thrive. We supported nearly 400 births in that beautiful space.

Then, in 2019, as my client base grew I realized that another, more central location was needed to adequately serve my clients. I felt that my location, 30 minutes south of Silicon Valley, limited the impact that I could make, so I took the leap of opening a new, larger space in a significantly more expensive area with the full buildout of a new location. My practice grew quickly with the new location soon to open, and I hired an office manager, a part-time midwife to help out, and I had a full-time student to work with me.

Then the pandemic hit and the practice doubled overnight. While some businesses buckled in COVID, ours was one that flourished. COVID lockdowns threatened everyone's feelings of safety: women were told that they could possibly be separated from loved ones and left to birth their babies alone, everyone was afraid to go to a hospital, and many pivoted to birth at home or in a birth center; Casa Natal welcome families with open arms.

Despite the growth this period brought to my business, it was a scary time; so many women were terrified of what might happen at the hospital, and fear of catching COVID while in a big central care center was a very legitimate fear. With the new location still under construction, we became a place of safety for these families in our original small space.

Red tape and new COVID protocols delayed the opening of our new space for months and the costs began to climb far above the original projections. I had to fire my original architect and find a new one mid-build. I felt like I was letting my clients down because the new space wasn't opening on time. I worried about the cost of all of the delays. I was having a hard time sleeping even when I wasn't up supporting clients all night in labor.

Managing a construction project, business expansion, and plethora of births during COVID, I often felt lonely. I had the wonderful support of my husband and family, but, as a female entrepreneur and business owner, I felt completely alone. I didn't have a support network to lean on and it felt very isolating.

At the same time, my son became sick and after taking him to the hospital was diagnosed with leukemia and a rare heart defect. He was admitted to the hospital just weeks before the lockdown. I couldn't believe what was happening. Suddenly the worries with the new project seemed worlds away. It was devastating.

Our third night in the hospital, as an infection raged through his body and we worried for his safety, a client called with a medical emergency. I stepped out of his room to compassionately help them navigate their crisis over the phone. As a midwife, you create a bond of trust with each of your clients. It was important for me to be there for this client in her time of need so that by having someone she knew and trusted, she would have less fear. Being a midwife and the source of help for a client in need doesn't change, even when I have my own crises. I must act as the safety net for the ones I love.

It was in the rush and chaos of all of these coinciding events, that I realized that the part time midwife I had hired was unreliable and I couldn't count on her in a crisis. I knew I needed more help. I was the rock of support for the women I cared for, but was searching for a life raft for myself. How could I still hold the standard of care for my clients, but also get the support I so desperately need? I was worried it wasn't possible to have both.

I'm confident this is a question asked by each and every successful entrepreneur as they navigate growing pains and a healthy work life balance: *How do I scale my business, but not kill myself in the process?* I was feeling like I was drowning. Suddenly a slave to a business I had once loved, and finding that I wasn't able to be there for my family. I was asking myself, "who am I doing this for, why am I doing this?"

It was an overwhelming and lonely place to be. I didn't want to let anyone down. My clients, my staff, or my family. I also felt, as a female entrepreneur, that I really didn't have peers to turn to for support. I didn't know any women that were running large, successful businesses. I honestly didn't even know what I needed. I just knew I needed help.

I had started my business to serve women, but I also did it for the freedom that owning your own business creates: I could work when I wanted and not have to adhere to a nine to five schedule. I could be available to my family to be the wife and mom that I wanted to be. But, as my business grew, I found that my freedom shrank. I couldn't even be available for my son when he needed me most.

I was in a cage of my own creation, a prison of my own design. Not because I didn't love the work, because I did and still do, It's my life's work to help create a safe space for women to have choice and be supported. But I didn't have a life-line to turn to in times when I needed help; I didn't have the community who understood the needs of running a business as a wife, a mom, a woman. I didn't have the support I needed to create support options or encouragement until I made the conscious decision to stop doing things alone and start doing things alongside other women who shared my same values. I hired midwives who are dependable and dedicated, and leaned into the rest and spaciousness that their support provides.

I also found a community of female entrepreneurs. I have always felt like I needed to be the rock of strength for everyone around me, the safety net as things crumbled for others. But, I realized that the way I did it was isolating and lonely. Everything began to shift when I joined this community that could support me in the areas where I needed help the most. Much like I do for clients, I began to realize that if I asked for help it wasn't weakness, it was a fulfilling, comforting, encouraging feeling; the safety net I myself had been missing. It finally gave me the tools that I didn't even know I needed.

Here's what I've learned in this ongoing journey of asking for support and flexing this painful muscle of vulnerability.

If I'm always the brick house no one gets to see inside. If I act only as the safety net, I will never learn to leap again. There's magic, opportunity, and way more joy in allowing other people to share and shine in their gifts, while I shine in mine. The beauty is in asking the right people for the right support. There's also magic in learning to trust that when you do ask, the right people will show up and deliver (no pun intended). My journey to this community of women, and this level of support and safety – both given and received – didn't happen overnight and that's okay.

I needed to approach it like I do with my functional medicine. Looking at the root cause of my symptoms, testing out what might be broken or missing, replenishing the nutrients or needs of support, and allowing the change to come. Holistic healing takes time, and I'm in it for the change.

Learning the skills of blocking time to work *on* my business and not always *in* my business has allowed me to reflect on ways to improve and grow. I can safely inch towards the edge of the plane without fearing the free fall will be the death of me, or others. Investing in myself and my business through community has also allowed me the freedom to be more creative and focus on growth. Hire amazing and talented people and allow them to shine in their own gifts, and your business will shine with them. Take the time to enjoy the process. Growth happens with failure and successes, but monumentally with failure.

For the woman reading this book, I want you to know that even if you feel alone, try to remember if you want to go fast – go alone. But if you want to go far – go together. Because with other sisters by your side, life will be more colorful and much more fun. Find your community!

We can all take action and authority when it comes to our health. For the women reading this that have health issues but are unsure what functional medicine is, these questions below are for you. Functional medicine treats root causes of disease and restores healthy function through a personalized patient experience. In the same way our businesses need care and attention, so do we.

Functional medicine looks way back into the events of your life to determine potential exposures and causes of your health issues. If you are facing some health issues that you are not getting the support you need to have them resolved, please reach out to me or a functional provider near you for answers.

Be aware that our current healthcare system doesn't understand this approach and that your health insurance will likely not cover much of your care. But this is the time that you have to determine what your health is worth. Functional medicine has the potential to create life changing healing and the potential to rid yourself of daily medications, for life; it's worth it to feel the best that you can. Here are a few questions to ponder when considering your goals for optimal health. Asking yourself these questions first will help you identify a provider that will also ask these questions and work with you to find the answers.

1. What do you hope to achieve in your health care journey?
2. When was the last time you felt well?
3. Did something trigger your change in health?
4. What makes you feel better?
5. What makes you feel worse?
6. How does your condition affect you and your daily life?
7. In order to feel better, how willing are you to modify your diet and lifestyle?
8. How confident are you of your ability to organize and follow through on your health related activities?
9. How much ongoing support might you need to make lifestyle changes?

ABOUT
MELISSA DEAN

Melissa Dean is a midwife and the founder of Casa Natal Birth and Wellness Center, located in the San Francisco Bay Area. As a functional and integrative medicine practitioner, Melissa combines her expertise in women's health with her midwife practice. She provides care in both allopathic and holistic health modalities to bring wellness to women in every stage of their health: including childbirth, transition to motherhood, maturing, menopause, and beyond.

Melissa's expertise has been featured in leading publications such as The Bump, Today's Parent, and The CheckUp. She has been a featured guest on leading podcasts such as Dear Doula, The Hypnobirthing Podcast, and The Go Deeper Podcast by Floka.

CHAPTER SEVEN
BRIEFCASE TO BABY BOTTLES

BRIGITTE BARTLEY SAWYER

I HAD MY FIRST CHILD WHEN I WAS 25 YEARS OLD, second child at 26 years old, and third child at 29. Yes, by the age of 30, I was already married for eight years with three children.

Throughout my time in college, my goals were career focused: to work as an executive in a corporate office while traveling the world. Quite honestly, getting married or having children weren't in my plans. In 1997, I graduated from a private liberal arts girls college and immediately started working for an automotive manufacturing company in Human Resources. I dove in hard and fast to my corporate bubble. Then, in 1999, I didn't get accepted into the graduate school of my dreams to pursue my masters in business because test scores on my GMAT were too low. For someone who is so goal oriented, I'm not going to lie, receiving that letter of rejection from the University of South

Carolina Graduate School felt like a punch in the gut. It was a mix of disappointment and frustration, like watching my dream slip through my fingers.

In 2000, I got pregnant with my first child. For someone who was originally so career focused, realizing that I was going to be a mother — even though it was our choice for me to step into the world of motherhood — was still an indescribable whirlwind of emotions, from excitement to nervousness.

In 2001, I resigned from my corporate job in Human Resources to be a full time mommy. I had absolutely loved my job, but I knew that this season of being with my baby was not one I could pass up on. I left the corporate world and never looked back, plunging full time into motherhood. Waving goodbye to the 8-5 to be a full time mommy was like stepping off a fast train, onto another fast train.

I was nervous leaving a job I loved, one that was steady and comfortable in every way, but the excitement of raising my child, being there for every milestone, outweighed it all. Motherhood is a whole new world of messy diapers, play groups, and bedtime routines that I grew to realize I wouldn't have traded for any office view or power lunch. And I didn't see it at the time, but denial into graduate school was the best thing for our family, and ultimately for my career later down the line.

Hear me out, I understand that not all women are called to be mothers and not all women are called to be full time moms; each of us has so many ways to live out our purpose in our own way. If you don't feel drawn to be a mom, or a full time mom, that is totally okay. This chapter is for the woman who does believe she is meant to be in the home, full time.

Transitioning from a corporate job to being a full-time mom can bring about many changes and challenges, but it can also be incredibly rewarding. Being a full-time parent allows you to be more present in your child's life and to play a more direct role in their upbringing. It can also give you the flexibility to manage your time in a way that works best for your family. However, it's important to recognize that this decision may come with its own set of adjustments, both personally and financially.

My world did a full 180. The reality of motherhood, especially in the early stages, is taking care of a tiny human and the baby's needs must come first. Having a 'schedule' really revolved around my tiny human. As our family grew, though, I began to realize that our children help me plan our days and nights. And as for the finances, just the diapers alone, add up quicker than you realize. Everything is an adjustment.

When I chose to become a full time mom, I didn't give up on my goals and dreams. I wasn't settling for something less-than. I didn't lose my identity or my independence, or so many of the things that society often tells women. I was taking on a new and different challenge: I made the decision to pour everything I had into raising our children. As women, we don't need to put an expiration date on our careers, and we have a lot of life left after our children are grown. Why are women concerned if they don't have a career they're not worthy? You can have that anytime you choose.

During the 13 years I was a full time mom, I channeled my passion for serving women and leadership into helping to start a Mothers of PreSchoolers Group, I taught bible study and weekly classes for women, I organized playgroups at various parks to give myself as well as other moms the support and community of other full time moms. It was less lonely than I could have ever imagined.

As a full time mom, explore some ways you can help serve other moms:

- What are some common challenges you observe in other moms around you?
- What are some of your strengths and skills that could benefit other moms?
- What resources, connections, or networks do you have access to that could be valuable for other moms?
- Are there local community organizations or groups where you can volunteer your time and expertise?
- How can you use social media to reach out and connect with other moms who may need support?

I am here to tell you that being a full time mom comes with immense purpose, even when the days of meal prepping, cleaning the house, and calming temper tantrums get mundane. There is an unexplained joy and fulfillment in motherhood. Being a full time mom can feel insignificant because of the humble work it requires. We don't get vacation time, business trips, or awards at annual meetings. Most of the time we don't get to eat our entire meal or even a full nights sleep, but in the work we do, we help our children learn people skills, to reconcile an argument with their siblings, we teach our children to manage their emotions, express their emotions with words and most importantly, we are their number one influence.

Seven more reasons that I have loved being a full time mom:

1. You get to spend more time with your children
2. You can control the environment in which your children are raised
3. You can instill your values in your children
4. You save money on childcare
5. You can be more involved in your children's education
6. You can avoid work related stress
7. Simply put, God told you to

Is being a full time mom just about crafts and baking? Not at all. Being a full time mom is challenging. It's tiring and can sometimes feel mundane and insignificant as you do laundry, dishes, carpool and don't bring home a paycheck. But being a full time mom matters. I believe that being full time may feel insignificant because we haven't trained our eyes, ears, and hearts to see God move in the ordinary. As we sit with our children, playing matchbox cars on the floor or play-doh at the table, we feel insignificant because we subtly believe that God only shows up in grand ways. And we know that society tells us that bigger is better. We can't hear His whispers through endless hours of pretend play, going to the park or playing outside. It's easy to believe that God only lives in the big: the company awards, the promotions. And let's not compare full time moms to working moms. Moms should be supporting, respecting, and encouraging each other no matter what their journeys look like. Being a mom is hard enough, creating a hierarchy of moms hurts the cause more than it helps. Your life as a woman, your life as a mom, means that your children are your heart, and a great significance to your purpose.

If you are a full time mom, or desire to be a full time mom, and you've struggled with this, my encouragement to you is to try and find peace in your decision. Consider taking the plunge into the previously unknown. There is honor and value in what you do for your family each day. If you truly believe you are doing what is best for you, your children and your family, then you are exactly where you need to be. We have one opportunity to raise our children, we have one shot at this, and for me, seeing them now at age 22, 21 and 18, I have full confidence that I made the right decision.

Finding ways to simplify my life as a stay at home mom helped me so much. Creating an eat/play/sleep schedule for my children and a weekly calendar to stay organized with our play-dates and library reading times saved energy and time. Having three children under four years old, I knew I had to structure our days.

A few mom tips that helped me:

- Create a morning routine - the start of your day will determine how the rest of your day goes. I highly recommend waking up before your children to get in your workout, shower, and quiet time to allow yourself to not only be prepared physically but to mentally declutter and clear your mind to prepare for your day. To this day, I am the happiest when I have my morning routine.

- Declutter your home - it will take time to declutter your home especially if you have years and years of random stuff in your house. Once a month, focus on one room in your home and release anything that you no longer use or no longer serves a purpose in your home.
- Have a cleaning routine - when your home is clean, you will be in a better mood, period.
- Create a meal plan, for your children, your family and for yourself - having a crockpot and airfryer makes preparing meals a lot easier (and healthier!) Having a meal plan will allow your week to flow more smoothly as well since meals are already planned out.
- Have "mommy time" daily - it's so important to create time for yourself during your day to relax mentally and physically. Take advantage of your child's nap time to read or to take a nap yourself.
- Spend time with like-minded friends - find other full time moms or a mom community to stay connected with other adults.

I do believe that my season of being a full time mom was part of my purpose. It brought me so much happiness being home with our children. It was an opportunity to dive all in on raising our kids. It gave me the confidence to weather any storm with my children.

In 2011, I went through a divorce; the catalyst to go back to work full time. Realizing that I was now fully in charge of my financial future, I decided to channel my passions of holistic health into a home based business. This allowed me to not only love what I was doing with an amazing team, I was able to create a full time income while continuing to be a full time mom.

Over the last 13 years, I have built a networking business team with other leaders that has grown to include over 115,000 associates. I have led various travel retreats, mastermind programs, and dove into personal coaching. I also became a licensed real estate agent and was in the top sales of my office my first year. Motherhood didn't interrupt these endeavors, it fueled them.

Plenty of women pause their career to be a full time mom and take time to raise their children. It's ok if you do too. Taking the plunge into motherhood doesn't mean that you lose the opportunity to have a career at some point in your life. I learned to swim in the currents of motherhood, and when the time came, I learned to swim again in the waters of a career. With family values strongly intact, I have been able to seek a career that allows me the flexibility to prioritize my children while providing for them, too.

ABOUT
BRIGITTE BARTLEY

Brigitte Bartley Sawyer is a multifaceted entrepreneur. As a certified facilitator for both microdosing and Hypnobreathwork, Brigitte helps creatives, entrepreneurs, and executives cultivate heart-centered leadership tactics, prioritize brain health, and improve physical, mental, and overall well being.

As the bestselling author of The Energy of Happiness, Creating Space and Signs, Brigitte has shared her journey with nutrition, mindset, spiritual growth, and breathwork for over 15 years. Her expertise has been featured in Yahoo Finance, HuffMag, LA Mag, Global NewsWire, and she was named one of the "Top 20 Female Entrepreneurs To Look Out For In 2023" by The NYC Magazine.

CHAPTER EIGHT
TAKING THE PLUNGE ON ME

AMY BARTKO

"BUCKLE YOUR SEAT BELT, PREPARE FOR LANDING." Blissfully unaware of what awaited me at landing, I followed the flight attendants orders, threw my headphones back in, and mentally prepared for what I thought would be just another business trip to Germany. I had no idea how much I *really* needed to prepare.

A few days prior the doorbell echoed through the house at precisely 10:07 am. Opening the door, I was met with an unexpected sight: a courier, surrounded by six imposing boxes, all for me. These boxes, a last-minute dispatch from my business partner, were meant to accompany me on my flight to Germany for what was supposed to be our grand showcase at the largest international baby and kid trade show. A project that was both my brainchild and my baby – not in the literal sense, of course, but as the passion project of a dedicated Enneagram Seven.

I was known for dreaming up grand ideas and seeing them through to both execution and financial success, but this time, the scale of the task was monumental. I had orchestrated everything from start to finish and sold the spaces, immersing myself completely.

Sitting on the plane, a world away from the comfort of home, with my six-week-old cradled in my arms, the weight of what I had undertaken hit me. The bustling cabin around me faded into the background as I longed for the familiarity of home with my husband, older son, and my newborn. Overwhelmed, fatigued, and enveloped in a profound sadness, I could only think, "I can't believe this is happening. I can't believe I'm on this plane, en route to Germany for a trade show."

The journey marked the beginning of a spiral into postpartum depression, a storm that seemed to unleash its full force the moment we touched down in Germany.

Schlepping the six boxes — along with my newborn, stroller, car seat, and all of the baby essentials packed into an extra suitcase — calling myself a hot mess would have been a colossal understatement. The situation took a turn for the absurd when, after arriving in Germany, I discovered that the boxes I had hauled from my doorstep in Phoenix contained my business partner's clothes, not products. Yes, her wardrobe had hitched a ride across the pond, courtesy of my six-week-old and me.

Shortly thereafter, I also learned that while I was juggling her luggage, our booth, and my newborn, she was gallivanting across France with a friend. I was beyond infuriated.

Spending hours on a plane, then hours setting up a booth with a six week old, I was beyond tired and overwhelmed. When

I packed up to head home, I realized I was packing up this part of my life and business journey. The road would end here.

The depth of emotional turmoil I experienced during that period was unprecedented, marked by a strong desire to return to the sanctuary of home. My expectation for support from my business partner was met with a stark reality: conspicuously absent support. Upon our return to Phoenix, Arizona, I claimed the maternity leave I so desperately needed and rightfully deserved, hoping time away would allow me to reset rather than need to rebuild. Only later did I learn of my partner's disparaging remarks to others: suggesting that I should feel "lucky" to have been compensated during my leave.

The shift towards self-prioritization emerged out of necessity, transcending mere desire. I knew that it was no longer possible to merely reset expectations, it was time to move on and rebuild. Severing ties with my harmful business partnership marked the first decisive step towards reclaiming my independence and establishing Chatterbox PR & Marketing, my current flourishing venture.

Despite the hurdles and legal battles that ensued to disentangle myself from my previous venture, the decision catalyzed a significant personal transformation. The steadfast support from brands and clients, coupled with the successes that followed, affirmed my value, talents, and aspirations.

Almost immediately after launching Chatterbox, I secured a contract with one of the leading trade shows in the baby and kids industry: the ABC Kids Expo. I became responsible for overseeing their PR, Influencer Marketing, and Social Media for several years — a testament to my established credibility in the field.

To fully comprehend the essence of embarking on a journey of self-discovery and personal transformation, it is crucial to explore the nuances of individual evolution that unfold over time. While distinct for each person, this path is woven with shared strands of introspection, bravery, and, ultimately, metamorphosis. Within the complex web of life, where roles are interlaced, and responsibilities accumulate, the core of one's being often becomes muted amidst the noise of duty.

For years, I, alongside countless others, trekked through the thickets of obligations, prioritizing the needs of my family, my business, and others above my own. Though personally mine, this tale echoes the experiences of many standing at the juncture of self-neglect and self-awareness. The quest towards self-choosing is both strenuous and illuminating, dotted with trials, epiphanies, and transformation.

Here's a truth I've embraced: choosing myself and daring to invest in my own potential unlocks the most empowered and authoritative version of myself, time and time again. This act of self-belief has cultivated confidence, bred tranquility, and ignited a sense of power within me. Everyday, this choice allows me to embody my true essence fully. Moreover, this transformation doesn't go unnoticed — the change radiates outward, capturing the attention of those around me.

The habit of consistently placing others before oneself is deeply rooted, especially for those of us juggling the roles of parenthood and partnership. This altruistic behavior, although commendable, often means that we sacrifice our dreams, desires, and health. Acknowledging this imbalance can be both shocking and enlightening, marking the first steps towards self-prioritization.

THE AWAKENING

My journey of self-discovery unfurled quietly amidst the rhythms of everyday life. In the realm of motherhood, the drive to nurture and protect my children was a natural extension of my being. This same fervor spilled over into my role as a wife, where I navigated the tightrope of supporting my spouse while holding onto my individuality — a task easier said than done. As mothers, we often find ourselves doing it all. Embodying roles that, if monetized, would astonishingly equate to an annual salary of $178,201, according to 2019 data from Salary.com, considering the endless list of tasks from household chores to financial management and beyond.

Before beginning my PR journey, I spent 12 years in medical sales. The 12-hours-a-day and intense corporate sales culture was finally too much for me, and I needed to pivot. I was trading a six-figure salary for presence in my children's lives, a move that was initially met with concealed resentment by my husband.

Despite his pretense of support, his true feelings surfaced over time. Yet, stepping away from my career did not mean stepping away from contribution or ambition: my side hustle in advertising sales, requiring merely 10 hours a month, generated an impressive $5,000 monthly — equivalent to a $60,000 yearly income, a figure not easily matched by other stay-at-home parents.

Certainly, focusing on the theme of choosing oneself and one's children to build a better foundation, we could adjust the passage like this: This venture in advertising sales transcended financial gains; it represented a deliberate choice to prioritize my well-being and my children's future. By aligning with a career that mirrored my skills and passions, I was not responding to an opportunity but actively choosing a path that promised a stronger, more fulfilling foundation for us all. This pivotal decision provided me with the work life balance I was craving and important for my family's well-being. It also demonstrated what I was capable of outside of a corporate setting. I was unknowingly trending into the waters of entrepreneurship. Still too new to take the plunge, but beginning to prioritize myself professionally and personally.

Within the corporate world, I faced the constant challenge of balancing support for my family with the pursuit of my dreams. Each compromise, each decision, seemed to push my aspirations further to the periphery. Yet, it was this very enterprise that catalyzed a profound personal awakening, a realization that for too long, I had placed my own desires and well-being on the back burner for the sake of others. It was a moment of stark clarity, a call to prioritize myself and question when it would finally be "my time."

The growing desire to step away from my time in corporate was met with an opportunity: a business venture that aligned perfectly with my interests and expertise in the baby and kid sector. Motherhood, with its intricate blend of love, concern, pride, and sacrifice, had often eclipsed my personal ambitions. The chance of a lifetime unveiled itself unexpectedly: a co-run PR agency specializing in juvenile brands, leading the charge in innovative kids' toys and products. This unforeseen opportunity was precisely what I had been unknowingly searching for, offering the perfect platform to intertwine my maternal insights with my professional ambitions seamlessly. I now know that this endeavor was merely a stepping stone to where I am now with Chatterbox, but at the time it opened up my world to entrepreneurship in a way I had never fully understood before. Germany was worlds away at the onset of this venture.

THE STRUGGLE AND TRANSFORMATION

The birth of my second son in 2013 became a watershed moment, blurring the lines between my personal life and professional ambitions with startling intensity. Juggling the responsibilities of the PR agency while embracing the demands of motherhood led me down a daunting path of postpartum depression. This arduous journey not only tested my resilience and sense of self but also honed my skills in advocacy, setting the stage for a profound plunge into self awareness and self care.

Choosing to prioritize oneself is an intricate dance, fraught with hurdles that challenge our perseverance, moral compass, and capacity for self-compassion. The strains in my business partnership, once a beacon of potential, morphed into a profound source of stress, illustrating the complexities of navigating personal growth amidst professional entanglements.

THE DECISION TO TAKE THE PLUNGE ON 'ME'

In November 2019, the dissolution of my marriage heralded a new phase in my quest for self-discovery. Choosing to leave, fueled by the realization that true growth thrives in a nurturing and respectful environment, was the bravest decision I've ever made. It sparked a profound exploration of what it means to live life on my own terms.

Looking back from March 2024, I can assert without a shadow of a doubt that leaving my 18-year marriage was the best decision of my life — a bold claim, but one that marks the point at which I truly found myself. My heart aches daily for my children, who struggle with the transitions between homes, expressing a preference to stay with me. Despite my desire to keep them close, I recognize the importance of their relationship with their father, especially given that they are boys.

These moments of choosing myself were monumental. Acts of faith where I gambled on my own potential and triumphed. Embarking on this journey of self-investment has been profound and immensely rewarding. If you ever find yourself questioning, "Can I do this?" Let my story remind you: Yes, you absolutely can.

THE EXPANSION OF SELF

The journey of embracing oneself unfolds through continuous growth and self-exploration. For me, this path entailed breaking free from a damaging business partnership and an unsupportive marriage, while courageously pursuing personal and professional opportunities I had previously overlooked.

By 2024, the fruits of choosing myself are evident in every aspect of my life. Chatterbox PR & Marketing stands as a testament to my entrepreneurial zeal and my pursuit of balance. Yet, it was the solitude inherent in entrepreneurship that prompted me to seek further growth and connection.

A pivotal moment in this journey occurred at Mom 2.0 in 2023. The decision to attend this conference, despite it coinciding with my precious parenting time, led to a serendipitous encounter that would profoundly alter my trajectory. In a breakout session led by the dynamic and knowledgeable Rebecca Caferio, founder of The Pitch Club, I was introduced to the concept of becoming a "6-figure podcast guest." Initially intrigued by the potential benefits for my clients — given podcasts' burgeoning status as the 'new Instagram' — I hadn't considered the implications for my own visibility and expertise.

Rebecca's world was a revelation. It not only encouraged but mandated self-promotion through a symbolic "permission slip," empowering me to advocate for myself in ways I had never imagined. This experience was transformative, granting me the confidence to assert myself as a thought leader and an expert in my field. Embracing this new perspective, I began to actively promote myself, resulting in noticeable shifts in how others perceive and interact with me. The feedback has been overwhelmingly positive, with many commenting on the impactful manner in which I'm now presenting myself.

I am a thought leader. I am an expert. And with newfound conviction, I'm ready to share my voice and insights with the world. This journey of self-expression and advocacy has only just begun, and I am thrilled to continue exploring the limitless potential of choosing myself.

THE ONGOING JOURNEY

The path of self-selection is an eternal one, marked by pivotal insights, daunting challenges, and profound personal growth. It demands a continual reevaluation of one's priorities, boundaries, and aspirations. My journey has moved beyond mere professional success and personal hurdles; it has become an embrace of my entire being — flaws, strengths, and all.

This journey has instilled in me the importance of self-compassion, resilience, and the pursuit of what truly fulfills me. It has underscored the truth that investing in oneself is not an act of self-indulgence but a cornerstone of authentic living.

The story of self-discovery and empowerment extends beyond the realms of business achievements or overcoming adversity; it's about the unending process of growth, healing, and recognizing that choosing oneself is the ultimate investment. As I continue forward, the lessons learned and the relationships forged cast a light on a path where my essence evolves from a whisper to a resounding voice shaping the narrative of my life.

Being immersed in Rebecca's world has profoundly transformed me. She has ushered me into the practices of self-care and healing; hypnobreathwork, sound healing, meditation, and Reiki. These practices have not only enriched my personal development but also deepened my commitment to mentorship and lifelong learning. Moving forward, my resolve to always bet on myself is unwavering. This journey has shifted my perspective on whom I choose to spend my time with. The ease of being a 'Yes' girl, habitually agreeing to everything, is a pattern I've left behind. The most authentic 'Yes' is the affirmation to oneself. Once you make that choice, your life will be irrevocably altered.

While this narrative is uniquely mine, its themes echo in the lives of many, illustrating the universal resonance of the journey towards self-empowerment and genuine change.

Here's my hope for you:

If you don't hear this anywhere else, here it from me now: You are worth choosing. I encourage you to take the plunge on yourself because that's where the true joy and expansion is found.

ABOUT
AMY BARTKO

Amy Bartko is a seasoned PR professional, a pioneer in influencer marketing, and the founder of Chatterbox, a PR company for family brands. She's recognized globally for building brands and promoting products for families, with a keen grasp on the unique niche of how to reach busy parents. Amy's clients have been featured in notable publications such as Forbes, BuzzFeed, and Vogue, among others, and seen on Today Show, Good Morning America and more. Amy's PR expertise has been featured in PR Week, The Marketing Strategy Academy Podcast, and more.

CHAPTER NINE
PLUNGING INTO 50

NATALIE BOESE

I AM A STORYTELLER. A big, fat liar. The stories I tell myself are short, but mean, and I repeat them relentlessly. The vicious way in which I don't spare myself a single nice word may be one of my least well known talents, or really, my biggest downfall.

If only I were just a villain in a movie like Cruella de Vil instead of the voice that's been in my head for the last 50 years. This talent is so spectacular, so cunning, I don't even know that I am doing it. The thoughts are less like words and more like a feeling that overtakes my body every time I want to do something I've never done before. And in some cases, this little voice creeps in even when I'm doing routine, everyday things.

When did the line between just playing for fun and playing to win get drawn not in pencil but in ink? As a kid we let ourselves colour outside the lines only until we are told that we are only supposed to colour inside the borders. If we colour outside of the lines, it's not a pretty picture; we always want to have the prettiest picture, right?

Elementary school progresses to high school and we all try to get the best grades to get into the best universities, and to get the best jobs with the most pay. Nowhere on that track did anyone grade our happiness, we just had to be the best at whatever we did. This is something I have fully subscribed to, but unfortunately, I was missing one thing. I never thought I was the best and I never really truly believed I could do it. I followed the march, but with the little voice in my head in tow.

Looking back now I realize that my entire life thus far had been a push-pull the whole way. Never fully diving into anything because my little voice would always hold me back. I love to write because I love the connection it gives me to other people, but what if they read it and they don't like it? What if I spend days, weeks, or months on something and people, well, they just. don't. like. it. Of course I don't know the true outcome of these self deprecating questions because of one of two things always happen:

One, I just don't put myself out there like that. And, two, people actually do like my writing but I never find out because I never stick around long enough to find out whether they did or they didn't.

How was hiding from myself serving me? Avoiding rejection by never fully trying, I would skim the surface rather than take the plunge. This surface skimming was a form of protection so that I could never, well, totally fail. It means, though, that I never really succeed either. It's like living in limbo, permanently. I have to admit: it sucks here.

I am a single mother of two boys, one with severe special needs. When my youngest son was born, his medical needs rocked our family to the core and changed the trajectory of my life forever. At that moment, it felt like the worst thing that ever happened to me. It was not the worst, but it definitely was the hardest. All of my needs were put aside for the "time being", but the "time being" turned into 14 years of feeling turned upside down. I felt like my life was out of control, that I was never able to plan and that I always had to be available for my son. Whether that meant I had to take him to his medical appointments, or be available if he was sick and needed to stay home from school, in my mind, my own life was not really my own. And in fact, I actually started to live that belief daily. It was a thought that transferred to my typical son as well. I felt like if he needed me, I should drop everything and address it, then and there. Everything began to feel like an emergency.

In 2016 one of my oldest and dearest friends offered me a plane ticket to go visit her and her family where they lived in New Zealand. I couldn't accept the offer. There was no way I could get away for more than a week, if even a week at all. I couldn't bring myself to ask my ex-husband to take the boys for such an extended length of time. The invite was for three weeks and I just couldn't make it happen.

The reason to decline was two fold: the time away from the boys and I was unable to accept such a generous financial offer from a friend. I should be able to pay for myself and I just didn't have the ability to accept. It was like a gray cloud would appear every time she offered. I couldn't see any way to make it happen.

But then seven years later something miraculous happened. My friend and her husband came back to Canada to visit their family in the summer of 2023. My boyfriend and I went to dinner with our friends and again, the offer to visit them came up in conversation. Without any control, my boyfriend accepted on my behalf. *'Oh shit. Oh shit.'* I thought, *'Now they expect me to come, and how on earth would I make this happen?'* I had work commitments. I had financial commitments. I wasn't ready.

Things were different this time, though. Both of my boys have moved out of my house. My eldest son had chosen on his own volition to go to boarding school. Simultaneously, an opportunity seven years in the making arose for my youngest: to move into a residential group home for children with special needs. I wasn't ready for either one to leave me at only 16 and 13 years old and I spent over a year grieving that change. I may not have been ready to take the full plunge and have both my boys leave home, but I am slowly easing into the waters of independence and choice, once again.

Suddenly the tickets for New Zealand were booked and the date was set to coincide with my 50th birthday. I was going to miss most of my birthday on the airplane shifting time zones. I showed up at the airport three hours early and still managed to miss my flight due to a delayed connection to Vancouver in addition to the little unknown fact that the New Zealand government now requires an actual visa for tourists. Road bump one. I did not let it deter me and I went home with a plan to come back in two days. This was my chance to take the plunge into something unknown, and I wasn't going to miss the opportunity.

I had a great time because all of the birthday wishes and messages came through as I was in the airports. I felt relaxed and a little more emotionally prepared to go. When I arrived, I found out that my friends Karen and Danny are a couple who live their lives to the fullest: they work hard, but they make sure to enjoy their lives equally. They had so many plans lined up for us and as we were traveling towards a winery, Danny commented that there was bungee jumping ahead. I have always said that I have a fear of heights. And maybe I still do because as I am typing this my hands are starting to itch just thinking of it.

Because of my fear of heights, I said there was no way I would bungee jump, so when Danny pulled the car into the parking lot, I thought he was kidding. The next thing I knew Karen, Danny and their very excited 11 year old daughter Emily were out of the car and on their way to the rock face overlooking the stunning Kawarau River. This was the world's very first bungee jumping site and it is 43 meters high, or 141 feet for more of a visual; it's like jumping off the side of a 13 story building. Talk about taking the plunge.

There was a running joke that they weren't going to jump, it was only going to be me. At first I said no way, but the idea was tempting. As I was debating with myself, a bus full of tourists came in for an appointment. If I were to go, it had to be now before the whole bus unloaded and lined up. So, I did something that the younger version of Natalie would never do. In a timid voice I said, "Okay. I'll go." At 50, I finally took the plunge.

I walked to the bridge and I looked at the team with the jumpers. This was so not for me. I asked the staff, "Have there been any accidents?" I was terrified.

"Whatcha mean, mate?" responded the guide.

"Well, I have a son in a wheelchair at home and I wanted to know if anyone has had an accident jumping." I tried again.

"Well, do you really want to know right now?" he responded.

And that's when I realized that I didn't. They bound my feet, they said a bunch of things that I was so scared I didn't even hear. All I heard was them say, "If you don't go on the first time I say, 'Five, four, three, two, one' it's only going to get harder to jump." So I nodded, and I wiggled my feet to the end of the plank since they were bound together with a long cable between them. I put my hands out to the side like a cross and I *smiled*.

"Five, four, three, two, one…" and at that moment, I knew exactly what to do, and why I was doing it. I tipped forward and dove into the air. It was amazing until the feeling of free falling felt like it would never stop. Then came the reverberation of going back up, nearly to the original height, only to have to fall all over again. It was beyond terrifying. But when I was finished and picked up in the river by a little yellow dingy I knew I was forever changed.

I knew how my life would look different when I got home, or even just on New Zealand soil. I was never going to look negatively at my life again. There was always a possibility and a way to create change. I wasn't going to let fear get in the way of reaching my goals, and I was now aware of what it felt like to feel alive. Instead of inching into the water like I had done so many times before, it was finally time to go all in and take the plunge.

Your life is short, no matter how many years you have on this earth. It's up to you to decide how you want to spend them. Do you want to wish your life away hoping that it will be different or do you want to let go of the fear of failure and keep trying, keep testing the waters?

Returning from New Zealand, I saw my life in a new light. I've got a lot of woobie blankets, you know, that little blanket that some kids carried around for way too long? It might have been your teddy bear, or even just a leftover scrap of material from the dear old blankey that your mummy gave you as a baby. As an adult, our woobie blankets can come in so many forms. We've got perfectionism, which as Elizabeth Gilbert says in *Big Magic: Creative Living Beyond Fear*, "I think perfectionism is just fear in fancy shoes and a mink coat, pretending to be elegant when actually it's just terrified. Because underneath that shiny veneer, perfectionism is nothing more than a deep existential angst that says, again and again, 'I am not good enough and I will never be good enough.'"

We also have old behaviour patterns. This might come in the form of relationships and choosing the same type of emotionally unavailable men, or hanging on to relationships with old friends just because they've known you forever. You don't feel great after seeing them, yet you don't let go of the friendship because you get to wear the badge of 'best friends forever.' A BFF that hurts to have is better than going out and forging new friendships that take effort, right? That would be a deep plunge into the unknown, trying to rebuild relationships and habits in your 30s or 40s.

This is not to mention our closets. They are filled with clothes that can range from size 6 to 18, yet we keep the full range because one day we pray to fit into our old clothes again, or plan to sell them on Poshmark to make enough to buy something even newer and better. What if our closets only held the clothes that we fit into right now?

What if you didn't save all the old jeans? I have a sneaking suspicion that if we were to be more forgiving with ourselves, we'd find that our weight actually doesn't fluctuate as much as we think. Instead of staring down our size 18 jeans with anger, or worshiping our size six denim, what if we were content with the clothes in the closet that fit us right now?

The woobie blankets continue. Some of us hold on to the past. We don't want to lose all the good memories, or the life that we once had. The tighter we hold on to those memories, though, the quicker they slip through our fingers. We will never be able to recreate the life that we thought was so much better than what we have now. And that's actually a good thing. If we could recreate our lives to match what we had, we would never get to experience anything new, never take the plunge into the future.

Each and every thing that we hold onto: behaviours, friends, partners, jobs, clothes, clutter in our homes, they are all associated with a memory. We keep holding on because we feel a sense of calm remembering the good times. We cling to memories and we start to identify with them. For instance, holding on to the perfect pencil crayon set we were given in the sixth grade when we were told we draw so well, surely one day we are going to become an artist. We repeat that story over and over in our head, but in reality, we were never great at drawing, we were just told that we were. Hanging on to those thoughts can also have us holding on to old goals.

Holding onto things that don't serve us may not always come in the form of something materialistic. You can hold onto old thoughts about yourself that no longer serve you. For instance, if you were ever told that you were not good at math because you failed a grade nine algebra test, that doesn't make it true. It just means that you failed that one test. It doesn't take into account what was going on in your life at the time, or any tests you've taken since then, not to mention other subjects that may be your strong suit. But if we tell ourselves a story (I suck at math) and we match it to an event (I failed a grade nine math test), it's only *then* that it becomes a problem.

If we just let go of old labels, and we don't worry about what we are or are not, and just take the next step forward, we will continue to get better at being our true selves. If I repeat that old story that I suck at math, I will start to believe that I shouldn't apply to any professions that require math because surely I will fail. Instead, behave as though we can do it and try until we can't.

Take notice and be intentional with your thoughts. Your thoughts will become your feelings, and your feelings become your actions, and your actions become your behaviours. Whatever we tell ourselves is ultimately true, so be kind and tell yourself a story that is an encouraging one, not one that is self deprecating.

What if the things you are holding on to are keeping you small but you don't realize it? For years, I convinced myself that going to New Zealand wouldn't be possible, until suddenly it was. If you let go of the story of telling yourself that you can't do it, or you let go of the clothes that no longer fit you, or the job that no longer serves you, and you focus that attention on diving all in on the things that excite you, imagine what you could accomplish. It's a pretty staggering thought because not only would you have more time in your life, you'd actually have more happiness and success.

Hanging on to what keeps you comfortable actually only holds you back from what you really want, and let me tell you, I have so many woobie blankets that they could fill a whole tickle trunk. It finally became time to let go of what was no longer serving me and making me happy. Letting go of these things has allowed me to lean in on the things that actually do make me happy. It has allowed me to untether, travel, and plunge into the unknown.

ABOUT
NATALIE BOESE

Natalie Boese is a lifestyle and digital organization expert, the founder of mac made simple, and a special needs mama. Natalie works with busy professionals to organize and optimize their systems so they can stop wasting time and start to generate more revenue, faster. Her digital expertise and organizational know-how have helped countless mamas and entrepreneurs to reduce overwhelm, create space, and find balance at home and in the office.

Natalie's expertise has been featured in Entrepreneur, Yahoo Life, Medium Magazine, LifeWire, and more.

CHAPTER TEN

PLUNGING INTO THE SACRED

CHRISTINA LUNA

"HM, WHAT IS THAT QUOTE? Write hard and clearly about what hurts?" He pondered as he hugged me, tears still wet on my face.

He had just granted me some time. Some peace. Space and reassurance that things were going to be ok. It sounded like something Hemingway would say, though my only reference point for Hemingway was a movie my soon-to-be ex-husband and I watched probably a hundred times before we divorced, called *Midnight in Paris*. The movie was about a modern writer who was in love with nostalgia, and dropped backward in time at midnight in Paris to a moment when he was able to meet all the biggies like Scott Fitzgerald and, obviously, Hemingway.

In my own way, at that moment, I felt nostalgic for our marriage. The sweet good old days when we watched movies over and over, reading through the plot-lines and feeling through the emotional layers. I loved him. I still love him. I still love everyone I have ever loved!

He said it best as he got out his checkbook, "We have a very unique situation," and wrote me a check for $5,000. A well of grief and gratitude burst when I received the support. Seven years after our divorce, seven years of complete silence, and he still believes in me. He still, after all the things we have been through, all the pain we caused ourselves and each other, *believes*. All the time that has passed, he still loves me too. And this love is mature. This love is not based on sexual needs and desire. This love is a true honoring of our humble and magnificent human selves. And he trusts I can write hard about it.

That small check for $5,000 granted the time, resources, and permission I needed to let it all go, to dissolve and unravel at a level I had never let myself fall apart to before. It was spring of 2020. I had spent the last seven years hustling to survive financially, too busy to really let it all fall apart, but when the shutdown stopped my massage business, I reached out and into our newly healing post-divorce friendship, for support.

He asked me about my book that he knew I'd started writing about the time we separated. I wasn't done with it yet. I couldn't finish it. But maybe the shutdown was the interruption my hustling-life needed to finally commit to completing my book.

When I say I unraveled, I mean completely. I went all the way in. Unapologetically, shame smeared and covered in toxicity, I dove. I had to find the core fear that was keeping me from publishing my story. No more trying to be wise, smart, or right. No more projection of blame. I had to face the fact that I was rescuing myself from my personal dragon of fear. And now I was willing. I was ready for the feast.

The plunge starts like this.

I dreamed of the trembling virgin tied to the post
awaiting the dragon.
She is being sacrificed to the feared one,

who will eat her alive.

This will bring safety, fertility, and peace to the lands below.

The dragon waits for her
in its cave.
The cave is the dark, dangerous places

we avoid entering.
We serve up the virgin at the mouth of the darkness, to
appease its inhabitant,
avoiding the chaos
and destruction
the wrath of the dragon might bring.

This is a myth. We all know there are no dragons. We all know there are no purely innocent humans. (Yet, I would invite you to ask if the exact opposite of both of these statements is actually true.) This is an archetypal memory or "truth" that we all have stored within our subconscious memory.

If we are honest, this sacrifice of the virgin to the dragon excites us all. We love the idea of fear, the idea of annihilation, and we expect that a knight, prince, or hero, will come and save the virgin. Her purity saved from the primitive desire of the beast, and made wholesome, preserved, by the domesticated masculine. Usually the knight's actions to save her create chaos and destruction for the town: The dragon will emerge from the cave, awoken and hungry, only to find the feeding post abandoned, robbed, unresolved. Enraged and filled with unquenched desire, it flies over the land below, blowing flames. Fields are destroyed, homes are burned, and the balance is broken by the wrath of the dragon.

Then there are questions. Does the savior want to possess the virgin for himself? Is she his prize? And who surrounds her?

There are onlookers. The ones who prophesied this union of the virgin and dragon. They brought her here to the cave in sacred ritual, feeling their own fear and desire, and in gratitude to bear witness to a new era that was to bring harmony and balance: The union of Wild Divinity. The dragon is summoned to consume her.

What does this mean to a modern serpent priestess who is just remembering this myth? What does it mean that I dream of seeing this virgin, sovereign, powerful priestess, erotically tied, with legs open, mouth and lips red and moistened by her tongue, eyes closed as she navigates her fear and desire from within, waiting for the dragon to consume her?

When the collective unconscious is ready to surrender to the wildness of divinity, the priestess is called to consummate this union to bring about the next era.

And how does she do this? She surrenders to the dragon within her. She allows her own desires to swell up, to draw her into her body so that she can be burned up by her aching longing. She surrenders to herself, free from judgment, with nothing to hide and nothing to prove. She expresses her ecstasy in ecstatic birth, for all to devour for themselves. To impregnate them with their own surrendered desire.

The freedom to be. Unbridled. Unchained.

Expression in the purest form.

THE LAST CHAPTER

"How will you know when you are done?" My editor asked. I have secretly named her 'The keeper at the 5th gate.' She posed the trick question as an invitation and a challenge.

I didn't have an answer. The truth is that I was trying not to admit that I was terrified of passing the 5th gate. I don't want to finish it. I want to linger in prose and swim in the ecstasy of work not published, not tarnished by the judgment of the public.

The temptress at the gate who had lured me almost to its threshold, had now become the dragon.

I saw my parents reading the first chapter and dying from heartbreak. After years of painful judgment of those *bad selfish girls* leaving their partners, they now see that their golden daughter is one of them, and they can't bear it.

I saw my ex husband, who I had worked hard to create a deep and loving friendship with, get offended and withdrawn because I didn't do our love and marriage justice and somehow made him look foolish or savage, or abusive, or some other thing that he is not.

I saw my current lover look at me in disgust and judgment, withholding his love, friendship, and cooperation, and making life for our daughter difficult and painful.

I saw D. and J. fighting and demonizing me to scapegoat their confusion over what was written about my feelings.

And, possibly most hauntingly, I saw that these people I love the most are the only ones who will actually read my book anyway. There is no real audience for my book. Nobody cares to read about the intricacies of my love life and the struggle to find true intimacy and the 'right' relationship.

The book, in my mind, is ultimately a failure, succeeding only in exposing my most intimate secrets to the ones I have guarded from them so carefully, now exposed and raw and proven in black and white. So really, all I have accomplished by finishing the book and publishing it, is that I have broken all of the bonds I care about the most, and I have nothing meaningful to show for it. I have impacted no one in a positive way, and now that people know the truth about my perception and life, no one trusts me or loves me anymore. I have lost everything. Everyone I care about.

I fall to my knees at the gate. I can't do it. The risk is too great. The book will remain unpublished.

I give my editor an impossible scenario in the answer to their question, "I'll know it's over when I actually meet my ideal love. The last chapter will be when the main character meets the ideal sacred masculine and he says something to her that she had imagined her sacred masculine would say, and that is how she knows it is him."

"So, I suggest you write the last chapter, before our next meeting. That way all you will have to do is fill in from where you are, to that ending point." My editor is a wise dragon.

"Ok YES I can do that! I will write the last chapter! I already know exactly how she will meet him. And maybe If I write it, it will come true! Though right now I can honestly say I am definitely not ready to meet a divine masculine. I think I would run away screaming if I actually met him. I would be afraid I am still too toxic and I'd fuck it up. Total self sabotage. But I can write about it."

Great. Fucking great. I am so full of shit. For four days straight after this conversation, I wake up early, against my will, feel the calling to go downstairs and write, and I tell the writing angels to fuck off. NO.

Instead I grab my phone and open Facebook. Not today, dragon. On the fourth day, a Friday, it's 3:30 pm, a gorgeous spring day, and I am in my dark room, in bed, crying. The sad sack is interrupted by a text from my ex husband:

E: "Hope you are doing well and feeling good! Such pretty days!"

I: "They are so pretty. Maybe we can take a walk later?"

E: "That would be nice! Just let me know. My schedule is open."

I: "How about 6 when it cools off a bit?"

E: "Sure, sounds great!"

I roll over and cry some more. Good, that gives me a couple of hours to pull myself out of this shit hole of despair and shower four days of filth off. I feel anxious. I assure myself that I can cancel our walk if I change my mind. It takes the pressure off enough to find a YouTube video to keep me company in the shower.

I thought I was through all of this after what happened last weekend. Life as a human is hard.

For sure, the high from my experience last weekend has worn off. Still it was an extraordinary experience. This is how it went:

Last Friday I woke at 5:00 am with an emptiness in my belly. I knew I had three more full days of alone in front of me, and I couldn't even sleep in. By 10:00 am I already needed to charge my phone. Whoa I have already consumed 5 hours of YouTube. I decided to take a break to charge my phone and get cleaned up. As I showered, I couldn't ignore the voice in my head that was reminding me over and over how much YouTube had been distracting me lately.

'Your weekly usage updates have measured it. You are averaging 8 hours a day. That means there are only about 4-5 hours of each day when you are not on your phone. Don't you think that is a bit alarming?' my internal voice screams at me.

'Well I listen to music too! It's not just YouTube and Facebook!' I retort defensively, wishing I had my phone playing in the shower to shut up the voices in my head.

'Hey, listen, we know you are using your phone to soothe yourself, and that's ok. We just want to know, what are you trying to soothe? What do you think you are getting from YouTube that you feel you can't get otherwise?'

As the warm water caresses my neck and back, I trace the question back into my past and observe. The content I watch the most are tarot readers. I guess I feel like they help me feel less uncertain about myself and my relationships, and sort of validate my intuition.

'Do you feel uncertain about your intuition?' I hear the little voice ask.

'Well,' I think to myself, *'yes I guess I do. I guess I am worried that there is something wrong with me. So I feel I can't trust myself.'*

Another question emerges from the steam: *What is the belief that makes you feel there is something wrong with you?*

I begin to spiral. If I was healthy and good, then I would be in a healthy and good relationship, not alone and lonely and separate. I *am* lonely and sad, so obviously there is something wrong with me. I am not smart enough to figure it out, so why would I trust myself?

All of the work I have done, writing this whole fucking book, the studying, the astrology readings and shamanic journey, and I am still fucking alone and sad. I am such a fucking fraud. So I watch eight hours of tarot readers to give me some kind of hope that something amazing might change. This morning they were all saying that this divine love will be entering my life soon."

'Do you see that you are addicted?' is the only response my conscious offers me in return.

'Yes,' I admit to the steam.

'Do you see that this addiction has gotten out of control?' another self berating question.

Yes, even now I can't wait to get out of this shower and get my phone.

'Do you see that you need help and you can't do this alone?"

"Fuck you. Yes." I say out loud.

The internal questions keep coming.

"So what are you going to do?"

I turn off the water and dry off. FUUUCK. I fucking hate this. I am addicted.

No I am not.

I can go downstairs and sit quietly just fine. I can leave my phone up here and just sit down there. I am not addicted. But what if someone texts or calls? Ok. How about I charge it downstairs but I just don't hold it or look at it? Then if someone wants to talk I will know.

I felt satisfied with my negotiation and prepared the couch for some sitting and doing nothing. Phone plugged in to the extension cord just out of reach, pillow under my knees, soft blanket. Let's do this. Maybe I'll get some food. And go to the bathroom. Ok. All set.

Immediately it sets in. I am so fucking lonely. I break open. "Oh *God* please! I am *so* sad. Please help me! I surrender! I don't know how to fix this! I don't know what I am doing *wrong*! I am just so fucking *sad*! *Please* help me! I just want to be loved! *Why* am I so fucked up!! It's so lonely and hard. I am so sad. Please help me. I surrender."

I keep my eyes pressed shut, and very gently, I begin to drift. I begin to imagine the image of a beautiful form. I fight off the gremlins that tell me that this is just my imagination. Years of Catholic church, pop religious culture, and idealized spiritual bypassing, tell me to ignore the vision, but I allow it until it crystalizes into a beautiful vision of Jesus. And my Lord, he is beautiful. The hair, the loving eyes, perfect five 'o clock shadow, white and rust colored robes, light shining from behind him or through him, I mean seriously, the whole nine yards. It's Jesus, and fuck you gremlins, just let me have this moment with my imaginary super hot Jesus, ok.

My imaginary Jesus comes and sits with me and I am immediately completely curled up and held by him. He's petting my hair as I cry. Just under my sobbing I hear him gently say, "It's ok, I am here. I have you. I love you, you are not alone, I am holding you and I won't let you go. No matter what, I love you. Everything you are feeling is ok, I love you no matter what. I am always with you. I have never abandoned you and I will always be with you. You are never alone."

"So why do I feel so alone and abandoned?" I beg.

"Oh, sweet girl. You have projected me onto others. You see me in those you love, and when they go away, because they are human, you believe that I have gone away. And you must feel right about what you believe, so you cannot feel I am with you. But I have been with you all along. I have asked you questions and loved you in any way you allowed me to."

Suddenly I saw that It was him that sent the shivers down my spine. It was him that asked me questions from beyond the curtain to help me see the truth of things. It was him, the benevolent voices in my head. I created an entire reality to experience him in the only way I would allow myself to experience him. I was jolted. "I have to write this down! I have to go!"

Jesus smiled and laughed. "You are doing it again."

"You have such a beautiful, brilliant mind, and do you see how it pulls you out of this intimacy with me? How you block yourself from receiving this love by believing you must do something with it? Leverage it in some way to gain the love of those who you would give your words to? Can you receive what it is you'd seek right now, in this present embrace?"

Weeping. Surrendering. Giving in to the ecstasy of the realization. I feel my entire nervous system unwind, vibrate, and relax. I feel drowsy and drunk in Jesus' embrace. My brilliant mind is finally at peace. I let myself fall asleep, completely unbraced, safe and trusting that the landing place is protected, sacred, and home.

That whole weekend alone with imaginary Jesus was magical. He was with me while we cooked, did dishes, sang, danced, and planned. Occasionally, he would remind me, "I will give you anything your heart desires! I want to build for you all the things you dream of! Just desire it and we will do it together."

A few times I thought about having a personal sexual experience with this newly idealized sacred masculine Jesus, and oddly I thought, I didn't even feel like it. I simply did not desire physical stimulation. I didn't want my phone either. It was actually difficult for me to desire much of anything except the presence and the joy of cooking and dancing and singing.

My conversations that weekend felt like testimonials. Several people reached out in their loneliness and I shared my experience uninhibited, knowing that my imaginary Jesus was with me.

By Monday, at my weekly appointment with my editor, I was still excited and high from the whole experience. I had awoken at 3:00 am that morning with a complete download of my entire codependent, love addicted, love avoidant tendencies. I had pattern mapped it all, including the legacy stream I had come from, through my mother and father, their parents, all of my lover's previous relationships and their parents, and how this legacy was now shifting with me and changing the trajectory of my children and future relationships. I saw it all.

It was detailed and succinct thanks to Mercury finally catching up to the Sun and conjunct my Chiron in Taurus at exactly 14 degrees; an astrological confirmation I made after the download was complete and guided by my personal Jesus. You can take the girl away from the astrology, but you can't take the astrology away from the girl.

My conversation with my editor was going brilliantly until she asked me the question that summoned the dragon, "So how will you know when you are done?"

So here it is. Another Friday and I am showering with YouTube, preparing to walk with my ex-husband and talk about how, even though he helped me with some cash, and encouraged me to 'write hard about what hurts,' I am still not brave enough to face the dragon and jeopardize the sweet connection we have been cultivating, among other things.

When I get to his house, the light and air and smells are beautiful. Ideal, in fact. He comes outside and offers me refreshments, which I decline.

"I had some water and a toaster strudel before I left, so I'm all fueled up!" I make a running in place gesture to add to the awkwardness, and we both laugh. This type of cheesy, awkward humor has been the lubricant that has helped us get steadily more at ease with each other over these past months. Breaking down the wall of seven years of complete silence following our divorce.

Over the course of the next few hours, we talk effortlessly. We talk about the book and the dragons of fear I am facing, if I really believe my parents won't love and accept me if they know the truth, how life is short and would we rather take unsaid and missed opportunities to the grave, or live them out boldly.

I notice that we see the truth of each other and still accept the humanness of us. We talk about what friendship means to us, about marble jars of trust (thank you Brene Brown for the visual) and how we can see our friendship deepening very slowly, and how that is ok. We have a unique opportunity to have experienced a marriage, a painful ending to that marriage, time apart to grow and get wiser eyes, and the gift of sharing that wisdom with compassion and humbleness. It's a beautiful evening.

By the time we are back to his place, it's dark and our conversation shifts to our son and my daughter. We are both realizing that the damage we have done to our kids is done. Our focus now must be on the present and taking responsibility for our role moving forward; own our part with them when they eventually face their own struggles. No matter what, they will have their own adversity. I tell him that with my daughter I am already noticing that I can give her what I wish my parents could have given me.

"Can you give me an example?" He asked.

"Well, This week for instance, she was isolating herself from her cousins, and got really sad because she missed out on me reading a book to them. When she discovered this, she was so hurt and sad and angry. She started throwing things at me and yelling. What I wanted to do was put her in time out and make her sit alone till she calmed down, but deep down I knew that wasn't what she needed. That would only invalidate her feelings and make her feel ashamed for:

A. Wanting to be alone

B. Feeling hurt

C. Getting mad

D. Being human.

So instead I finished the story, picked her up, kicking and screaming, took her outside where we could be alone together, and I held her.

Over the punching and writhing and screaming, I loved her and said, 'It's ok, I am here. I have you. I love you, you are not alone, I am holding you and I won't let you go. No matter what, I love you. Everything you are feeling is ok, I love you no matter what. I am always with you. I have never abandoned you and I will always be with you. You are never alone.'

Until she just curled up in a little ball and let me hold her and love her. Until she knew she was loved unconditionally, no matter what."

Shivers took hold of my body. Whoa. In my mind's eye, I saw myself being held by Jesus on my couch as he gave me those exact same words when I was so sad. My thoughts lingered further then, to my conversation with my editor, *"how will you know when you are done?"*

"I'll know it's over when I actually meet my ideal lover. The last chapter will be when the main character meets the ideal sacred masculine and he says something to her that she had imagined her sacred masculine would say, and that is how she knows it is him."

I saw that I have been the sacred one all along. I delivered that sacred message to my little girl. I heard myself say it out loud, exactly what I had imagined my sacred masculine saying to me. And I declared that I would *know* it would be him when I heard him say the things I imagined!

Profoundly as I have now typed this last chapter, I myself have said it three times.

"Hey, are you okay?" my ex-husband asks. Noticing I am having some type of profound soul experience that has me with who-knows-what kind of look on my face.

"Oh, hahaha, yeah. I'm just remembering some stuff that happened last weekend."

"Cool. Well, Goodnight." We hug and I get into my car. I drive a while on the side streets, giving myself time to process.

Holy shit. Did I just find the thing? The core of the thing of all the things?

Yes. I think I did.

Will I forsaken myself? Will I finally accept with full faith that Christ is alive within me? My Christhood is the divinity I have been waiting for, that has always been, and has never abandoned me. Will I abandon this truth again to experience the pain of separation, imagining that this love must come from some "other," and continue the seekers journey for "them"?

I am human. So it's possible. Let's be real.

But for now,

I remember.
And I will share this story.
I will face the dragons
of fear
that guard the gates
to true intimacy
with myself
and others.
And I have.
And so it is.

My name is Christina.
Little Christ.

And I sometimes forget
that I love myself.

It took a lot for me to remember this
AGAIN.

I'm a sacred human,
so that is ok.

And you are a sacred human too.
I hope you remember
now with me.

Thank you for bearing witness
to this life.
I see you
and I love you.

You are never alone,
even when you believe you are.
I promise.

We are,
at our core,
pure divine love.
This is truth.

Remember.

ABOUT
CHRISTINA LUNA

Christina Luna is an astrological mentor, a sustainable business guide, and an artist. Her work is rooted in the understanding that our presence is our purpose and mission in life. Growth, happiness, and success come when we act in accordance with our somatic truth. Christina helps entrepreneurs live fully, lead eloquently, and find alignment with their soul and their life's work.

CHAPTER ELEVEN
TAKING THE PLUNGE ON SOBRIETY

MICHELE WATERMAN

I DIDN'T KNOW WHAT WOULD HAPPEN IF I GOT SOBER. But I did know what would happen if I didn't. It's been twenty-two years and counting without a drink. That means that my kids have never seen me drunk.

The reality is that I have another drunk in me. I just don't know if I have another sobering up. I took the plunge more than two decades ago with the hope that I could become the woman that I am today.

The truth is that when I stopped drinking, I was still getting away with it effortlessly: drinking excessively, many evenings to oblivion, while producing, pleasing, performing, and perfecting a life that looked amazing from the outside. I had amassed success in every way that is measured by society's standards. You would never know from looking at me that I was dying on the inside.

My last drunk was June 20, 2001. I had my first drink at age 13 in a small town north of Napa Valley. I had my last drunk in that same town at age 32. My moment of clarity — the moment when I realized I no longer had control over my drinking — came on a Thursday in my grandparents' home where I spent every summer since I was four years old. I had no intention of drinking that night and yet there I was bent over the porcelain god while the room spun and I said out loud, "How did I let myself get like this?"

Alcohol was an acquired taste that I tolerated because I loved the way it made me feel. At age 13, I didn't set out to become an alcoholic. I wanted to fit it with the older kids that were drinking. I wanted them to like me and think I was cool. I remember that drink like it was yesterday; warm Budweiser bubbled and burned the back of my throat and produced a warming effect in my belly almost instantly. Soon I felt relaxed, uninhibited, and unafraid that my grandfather might wake up and realize I snuck out to partake in what would be the high I chased until alcohol turned on me.

My last drunk (and blackout) was preceded by two years of doing everything in my power to drink less. And as I drank less, I thought about drinking more. This is called "controlled drinking." It's that inbetween phase many people explore when faced with the realization that they are drinking more than they would like to admit, but fret over — and even grow to fear — the idea of giving it up all together.

For most of my life, I drank the way I wanted to: before, during, and after the party; I always hoped it would never end. But when you drink as much as you desire, whenever you feel like it, and justify your cocktails with your work ethic and hard-earned lifestyle, you don't have to bump up against "choice". So, I declared myself a party girl – and prided myself on being the life of it!

I convinced myself time and time again that I could continue drinking. I never missed a day of work or a workout. I was a high-performance sales executive in the top 2% of a publicly traded corporation. I was making six figures. I was married to the love of my life and we had a beautiful baby — a planned blessing. We lived in a huge house in a gentrified, hip town in Silicon Valley. I drove a luxury imported vehicle. We traveled all around the world on trips we garnered. We had the right friends in the right places…I mean what's the problem?

My (then) husband and I got married in Napa Valley, an idyllic venue for our wedding and a gorgeous get-a-way to celebrate our second wedding anniversary. We made the trek up north from Silicon Valley on a Thursday to give us time to get up and over Saint Helena Mountain so that we could have some family time with Jace, our 13-month-old baby, and my folks before we headed back over the hill to enjoy wine tasting and a romantic weekend for just us.

Drinking was not on the schedule; my drunks were planned for the weekend. It was a sunny, warm day, the first day of summer. We walked down to the lake to take Jace in the water and splash around before dinner. As the afternoon persisted, I slid open the tiny white and blue cooler my mom had brought down to the beach, hoping to find something to quench my thirst. Sure enough: five waters and one, ice cold Corona. I started to salivate.

'*Wait,*' I thought. '*I don't even like beer.*'

And yet, I found myself asking, "Hey mom, did you bring down a church key?"

"Oh sweetheart, I'm so sorry I forgot," My mom replied.

"Oh, no problem," I said back to her. "No biggie, I'll just drink water!" and I proceeded to do just that.

I blew up Jace's floatie and out in the lake we went. I wanted to enjoy my time in the lake with my family, but all I thought about was how fast I could get back to the house, find a church key to open and chug that Corona. The idea of drinking beer consumed *me* before I even had a chance to consume *it*. Rather than basking in the warm sun and splashing with my child in the water, I was entirely overtaken by the idea of drinking a beer.

Several hours later, I had my way with it; glug, glug, glug, glug, glug, down the hatch it went. Followed by,

"Hey, Mom, do you have any red wine?"

"Yep. Go in the room where we put Jace's Pack and Play — the wine racks in there, sweety."

Was it a fancy bottle of merlot or a pinot noir? Who cares at that point. I was drinking for effect. Once the cork was removed, I poured that first glass and gulped it down. There was no smelling. No savoring. No tasting. No noticing the legs running down the inside of the glass. Sure, I knew all the things to talk about so that I appeared to be a wine connoisseur, like the people I met in Aix-en-Provence during my year abroad. But by then the only thing I was appreciating about the wine was its high alcohol content.

One. Two. Three glasses of wine were downed in quick measure and I was ready to open another bottle, only to find out that my mom had just put Jace down for bed in the room where my folks kept the wine rack.

I wanted to be a present mother. A good mother. A mother that cared more about her baby's sleep than my need for alcohol. So, I prioritized Jace's sleep, dropped the idea of more red wine, and switched to the 151 Bacardi my dad kept in the garage and chased it back with piña colada mix. As we all sat under the stars, talking and carrying on, I could not figure out why I didn't feel drunk after all that I consumed. I drank, and drank, and drank, and nothing was happening until it all hit at once.

Once back inside, the room started to spin and I felt a familiar swell of nausea balloon in my stomach. I made my way to the bathroom and assumed the position. I got down on my knees, flipped the toilet seat lid open and prayed I could purge myself of the spirits that I had so eagerly guzzled. My mom walked in to check on me; she rubbed my back and reassured me that I would be okay as I slurred, "How did I let myself get like this?"

The truth is: I didn't let myself get like that. I had lost my ability to predict what would happen once I took that first sip. I had lost my choice in the matter. So I stumbled across the back porch and flung my body onto the bed, hoping and pleading with a higher power to please make the vicious vertigo cease.

The shame of what happened next will be forever etched in my memory. I came around early the next morning to my then-husband's arms stretched out holding our child for me to take into my arms as he reported: "Michele, I can't do this anymore."

My stomach turned with nervous anticipation. Was he going to divorce me right before our second wedding anniversary? So I said, "You can't do what anymore?"

"I can't take care of Jace alone anymore, Michele. Jace was crying for you all night while you were passed out."

And the only thing I could think to say in that moment was the truth:

"Craig. *I am an alcoholic.*"

To which he said, "I know, honey."

I continued: "I need help. I am going to start going to meetings." And I meant it.

PLUNGING INTO SOBRIETY

I drank alcoholically for nearly twenty years. I had no reason to believe I could get and stay sober. My entire life provided evidence to the contrary.

I had my first black out at age 13. Looking back, I had crossed that invisible line in high school and lived a double life for decades. I was an athlete and a weekend warrior until hangovers outpaced my performance in sports. I sought out people that performed, played, and partied as hard as I did. I found myself in corporate cultures that rewarded hard work and success with booze and substances, which ran rampant in high performance environments.

The scary thing is that I drank alcoholically for 19 years without a whole lot of consequences. Consequences like DUIs, losing jobs, destroying relationships, getting into accidents or other predicaments that most people require before they become willing to give up alcohol.

The reality for many people that drink to excess like I did is simply this: *drinking is our solution to our problems with living.* It's liquid courage. It helps us take the edge off and is that magic elixir that enhances a life well lived.

TAKING THE PLUNGE ON SOBRIETY

Rather than go into treatment, I went right into a fellowship with other people getting sober, and I picked up the toolkit that was provided. I worked on the wreckage, addressed the things I did and didn't do, as well as the things I said and didn't say. I got to work and became willing to make amends for my whole life.

Taking the plunge on sobriety meant that I committed to myself that no matter what, one day at a time, I was not going to pick up a drink. I conceded to my innermost self that I was a pickle, and I was never going to be a cucumber again. I pretended I was at the county fair with a finite amount of drink coupons and mine were all used up. Drinking needed to be an option I took off the table because there would always be a reason for me to drink; my first year sober taught me that. Where alcohol was concerned, I accepted the idea that I had an allergy to it just like penicillin.

My lived experience painted a very clear picture for me: I could not safely take a sip and predict what would happen next. I was a wild card when it came to alcohol. Once I consumed any small amount, the phenomenon of craving would set in and the obsession of the mind would take hold. With drink in hand, I would be off to the races, and you can bet on the fact that I could never win where alcohol was involved. So, the best option for me was complete abstinence.

Some get sober and gain back all they lost while drinking. But for some of us, we get sober and then life explodes and gets way harder before it gets more manageable. We don't all get sober and earn prizes. Some of us get our teeth kicked in by life in our first years of recovery. That was my story. I got my ass handed to me.

SOBRIETY: YEAR ONE

My newfound sobriety bolstered my confidence. I discovered an internal strength inside myself I didn't know existed. In the first few months of my recovery, I discovered a resilience and resourcefulness that fueled my determination and dedication to become the wife, mother, and leader that would figure out how to suit up and show up under any condition, ready to face life on life's terms no matter how hard, no matter how horrific, no matter how unprepared I felt to face what would soon become my reality.

I got pregnant with our second child in the first few months of sobriety — another planned blessing. I worked the program and did all the things to clean up the fallout of my past. I was in grad school getting my master's in counseling psychology, chasing after our toddler, running a household, going to meetings daily, and doing my best to keep the love alive in our marriage as I changed my life for good.

Then, at nine months sober and seven months pregnant, I got the call no wife wants to get: that my husband was airlifted to San Jose Medical Center after a severe motorcycle accident. The doctors were ruling out a broken neck. Craig had lost consciousness. We didn't know the extent of his injuries, but when I waddled into the hospital, I was greeted by a social worker which is never a good sign.

She led me into a room where Craig was laid out flat on a gurney, neck immobilized by a stiff plastic brace. I hurried to his side, my belly protruding several inches in front of me, coming up right to his line of sight. From his peripheral vision, he regarded me with visible disorientation, brow furrowed, blinking hard. He did his best to look up at me and remarked,

"Oh my god, honey. You're so fat. Are you pregnant?"

I burst into tears. He started to cry as well, because he had no memory of my pregnancy, no idea who the president was, or what year we were in.

"Where is Jace?" He asked me, beginning to panic, "How old is Jace? Where is Jace?"

I lost the love of my life that day. Craig looked the same on the outside but he never returned to the man I married. He didn't work for five years following his accident, meaning that not only did I have to take care of a toddler that wasn't typically developing and a new born baby, but I was now responsible for caring for a teenager of a husband. I was emotionally alone and operating like a single mother inside the shell of a marriage.

I thought I had hit rock bottom, but the floor continued to fall out from underneath me.

The day before my second child was due, my dad flatlined. As it happened, he was already in town, having planned a strategic visit with his cardiologist around the date I scheduled to go in for a C-section. It was with this cardiologist, during a routine treadmill test that my dad's heart stopped. If this had happened almost anywhere else, he likely wouldn't have been able to be resuscitated. But thanks to the quick intervention of the cardiologist, after a few vigorous passes with the defibrillator, his heart had begun to beat again, and he was rushed to the same hospital Craig had been airlifted to not three months before.

While my dad was hooked up to an array of machines, a pacemaker put in his heart, I was at another hospital just across town having a C-section. There, my daughter Alyssa was born with a heart defect.

As I juggled the stress of caring for a newborn susceptible to heart failure with taking Craig to neurologists and therapists to assist with all that goes into rehabbing a TBI, our eldest child Jace was diagnosed with full spectrum autism at UCSF.

In those first months of sobriety, I had more excuses to drink than I did reasons to stay sober. Lucky for all of us — me, my family, my marriage — my reasons for staying sober mattered more to me than my excuses, and they weren't going anywhere.

THE NEXT RIGHT THING

The timing of my plunge into sobriety was as fateful and vital as the timing of my father's flatline. It was not a decision predicated on my life falling apart, but rather was a serendipitous preemptive measure, an intentional choice to veer out of the vicious cycle that dominated my parent's marriage, and made my own childhood so chaotic. On the first morning of my last four day hangover, my father told me that he would never drink with me again, as I had drunk him, a seasoned, unswerving alcoholic, under the table.

In that moment, I saw clearly the road before me: a road too close to my father's own life path for comfort. If I decided to continue down that road that hot day at the end of June, I would not have been in a place a year later where I could navigate my family out of the mess we found ourselves in.

Instead, I made a commitment to myself and to my family that I would not become the parent that had once hurt me. I refused to let alcohol keep me from self-reflection. I would not become a parent that says and does things that requires my kids to abandon themselves because they're not safe to be seen, heard, and known, in our family system.

It was this commitment that blazed the trail for me to be a medical advocate for my entire family, starting two 501c3 nonprofits to promote equity for people that identify as neurodivergent, specifically autistic and dyslexic.

I combined my own sobriety with decades of experience in marketing and sales, and turned it into advocacy, grassroots activism, and community impact. I learned how to be of service and leverage my experience, strength, and hope to pass on what was freely given to me. Despite what I have gone through, I know that I have so much. I have figured out a way to help people and then ask them to pay it forward once they get the help they need. This is how we use our voices for good.

When I bet on myself and took the plunge to stop drinking one day at a time, I had no idea what was coming around the bend. I had no idea that the timing of me committing to my own recovery would keep me from passing down the patterns of abuse and neglect that my parents, even if unwittingly, passed down to me. All I knew for certain was that I would do everything in my power to at least do the next right thing, to take one small step away from who I had been and towards the woman I hoped I could be.

'No matter how hard life is today,' I would tell myself, *'I am not going to pick up what provided escape before.'*

I slowly became resilient and confident in my own capacity to learn, to grow, to change, and to commit to becoming all that I can be. When I face the wreckage of my past, I know that the things that happened to me weren't my fault, but my recovery is my responsibility.

FAMILY SYSTEMS: BREAKING CYCLES OF TRAUMA

Growing up in an alcoholic home left indelible marks on my psyche and soul. We looked like a perfect little family out in our community but behind closed doors, chaos and confusion were my constant.

Make no mistake, there was love in my house. My dad was a good man. I know for a fact that he would walk through fire for all of us. He was funny and playful, dependable, and reliable. He loved music and being in nature. He was good at everything and there wasn't a problem he couldn't solve. Everyone loved my dad — the life of the party, the template for the uninhibited free spirit I would become. His behaviors were also unpredictable, unkind, and, at times, unacceptable.

At 18, he joined the navy and was shipped off to Vietnam. War compounds and amplifies adverse childhood experiences. He too grew up in a home of addiction and abuse. I know now that my dad was a wounded man that never got the help he deserved to reconcile what happened to him.

For years, I used the progressive nature of his drinking to become the yardstick I measured myself against. In my mid-twenties, I sought out career counseling trying to make sense of a toxic work environment. I surprised my counselor and myself when I blurted out, "I just can't be an alcoholic, I just can't be like my father!" I had been asked about my work life, but clearly there was something brewing more deeply.

Denial allowed me to gag down the truth: I had already become who I promised myself I would never be. It would take seven more years of running from myself before I was ready to take the plunge and put down alcohol for good.

Today, I am the adult child of an alcoholic, and I am in recovery from everything that gets in the way of honoring myself. And although I haven't had a drink in 22 years (and counting), every day I take the plunge and commit to not only keeping the plug in the jug but to go to any lengths to own myself and all my choices.

Walking away from alcohol was not enough for me. The reclamation I was after required me to face myself and all the behaviors and coping strategies I learned in my family system. I learned that alcohol was just one of the tools, not the whole shed. What I discovered was that my external success masked my pain that I numbed with not just drinking, but exercising, spending, and achieving to excess, as well.

My sense of self was governed by the approval of others. I was a goal setter and goal getter that seemed to be able to achieve anything I put my mind to. Yet over time, I was like a rat on a wheel, going round and round with increasing speed, but getting nowhere fast in my quest to prove my worth and value. Achievement for achievement's sake became its own addiction. In my obsessive quest to be the best, external validation was the oxygen I breathed to stay alive.

My recovery has largely been an unlearning process. Taking the plunge into the unknown has been a wild and bumpy ride for sure. Yet the peace and freedom I know today – this joy of truly living – is a priceless gift I would not trade with anyone for any amount of money.

COURAGE IN ACTION

If my road to recovery has taught me anything it's simply this: It takes truckloads of courage to create lasting change and the great news is that courageousness can be cultivated.

Today I take 100% responsibility for how I show up in the world to break the chain of addiction, to untangle myself from patterns of codependency, people pleasing, and perfectionism. I am all about taking massive action and making changes in how I live my life. I do not shame or abuse myself or my loved ones in any shape or form. That's how we prevent trans-generational trauma from being passed on.

Here's what's true: We are magnificent, powerful, and capable of becoming who we know we were always meant to be. We can reconcile the pain of our past. We can reclaim our wholeness. We can come home to ourselves. We can. I am doing it and you can too.

We don't magically gain confidence and then go out in the world to pursue greatness. We go fearfully out in the world and do what scares us. We dip our toes in the water to test the current, then we jump in – a courageous act of bravery. That creates confidence. Being brave builds confidence and then our confidence cultivates more courageousness. This feedback loop fuels us to do hard things again and again.

Often, the problems of today appear insurmountable. They are not. It's in these moments of challenge that we gain the grit and capacity to persevere. It's important to reflect on the evidence of your lived experience. Look at what you've already overcome and accomplished.

Give yourself the gift that only you can truly give: the permission to create a whole new way of life for yourself. To create lasting change, you must face yourself and your life and consider your choices. Change begins with getting real and right sized — by getting rigorously honest with who you are compared to who you know you can be. Coach the gap. The truth has the power and potential to set you free if you're willing to be open minded about the possibility of what could be when you commit to taking action to create a whole new life on your terms and timeline. This is the jumping off point from which you take the plunge.

It's time to unlock your courage. It lives inside of you. My invitation is to go all in on you. Bet on yourself and your growth like you can't lose. Start with small incremental changes which will build confidence and then start stacking habits.

Take the plunge, and when you do, you'll build capacity, competence, and the confidence to take more chances on yourself.

Now Go. Get out there. Be willing to be in the messy middle. Be willing to fail forward. You got this. Let's be courageous together and create lasting change.

ABOUT
MICHELE WATERMAN

Michele Waterman is a writer, mental health and disability justice advocate, and the host of the Courage Unlocked podcast. She is a nonprofit business strategist and consultant. Her background as a founder and executive director for Mission Valley Preparatory Academy and The Autism Education Network has equipped her with a high level understanding of how to build and run 501c3s that create real impact.

Her third and newest nonprofit, Use Your Voice For Good, is an interdisciplinary 501c3 rooted in the guiding principles of social work and a culmination of Michele's experience running nonprofit organizations, advising family foundations as they grow, and coaching founders. From resources for crowdfunding, to founder support and grant and scholarship resources, Use Your Voice For Good is the homebase for the nonprofits of tomorrow.

Michele's work in the nonprofit space has been featured in The San Jose Business Journal, NBC San Jose, as well as on stages for important policy work, nonprofit fundraisers, and more.

Made in the USA
Columbia, SC
31 August 2024